Frontispiece
**Initial Series written with full figure
glyphs. Stela D, Copan**
A1: Introductory glyph. Patroness is the
moon goddess. Fish replace 'comb'
affixes at sides. B1: 9 *baktuns*. A2: 15
katuns. Note jawbone for 10 on head of 5
to form 15. B2: 5 *tuns*. A3: 0 *uinals*.
Hand on lower jaw of figure is 0 symbol;
a realistic toad represents the *uinal*.
B3: 0 *kins*. Again the hand on jaw to
represent 0. A4: 10 *Ahau*. B4: the night
sun, as lord of night, rises from ground
with jaguar skin (night sky) as his load.
A5: 8 *Ch'en*, the month position. B5:
meaning uncertain. *After A. P.
Maudslay.*

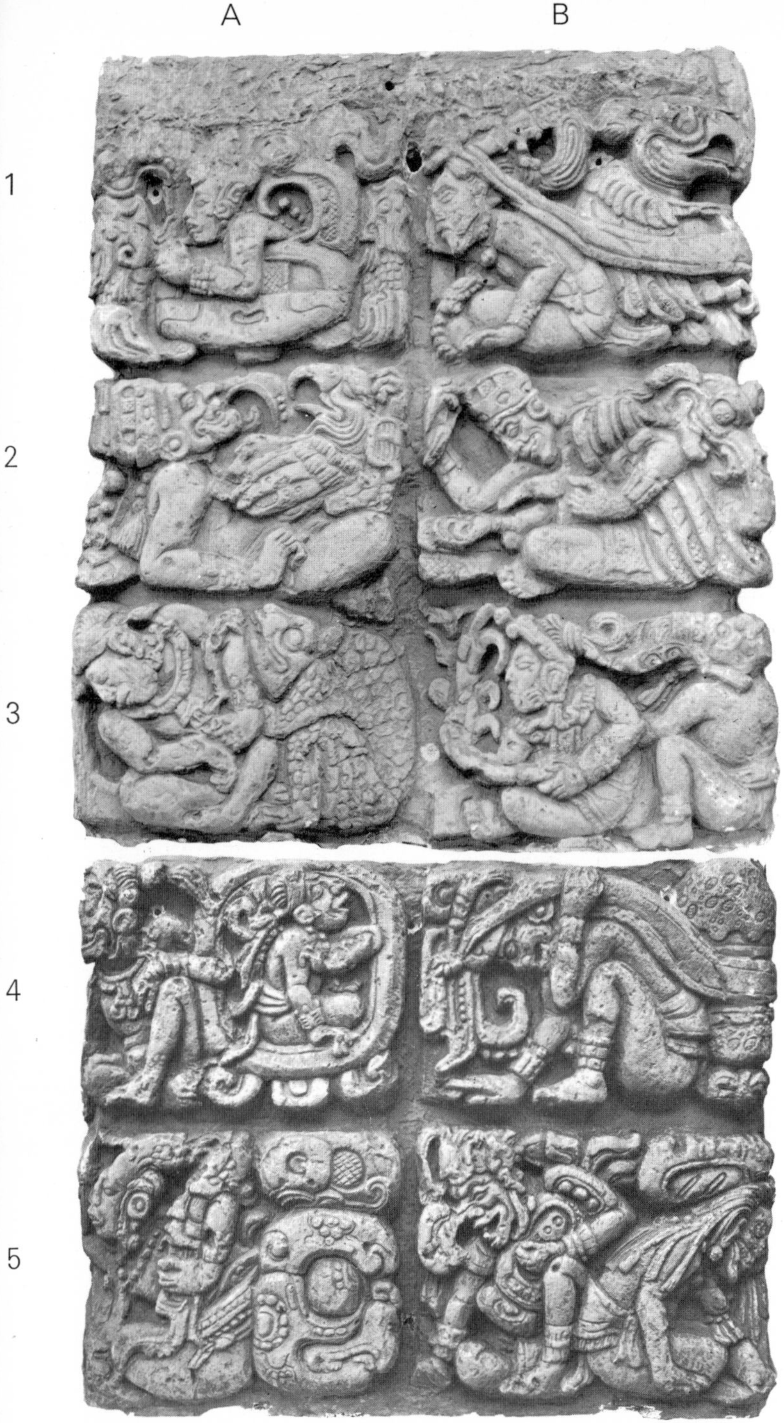
A
B
1
2
3
4
5

MAYA HIEROGLYPHS WITHOUT TEARS

J. Eric S. Thompson FBA

Published by the Trustees of the British Museum 1972

© 1972 The Trustees of the British Museum
SBN 7141 1520 7
Printed in Great Britain by Shenval Press

The Ethnography Department
is at 6 Burlington Gardens London WIX 2EX

Contents

Introduction   *page* 9

A brief history of Maya writing   20

The formation of Maya hieroglyphs   27

Landa's alphabet and the task of decipherment   31

'Rules' of glyphic composition   35

Wider considerations   68

Exercises in decipherment   70

References   81

Index   82

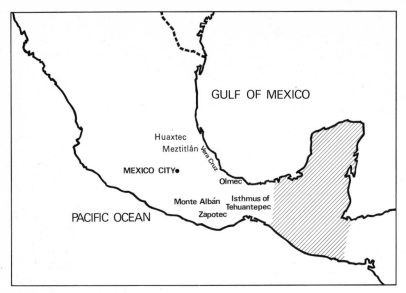

Above
Map of Mexico, Guatemala and adjacent
countries. The shaded area indicates the
Maya area shown in the detailed map
on the right.

Right
Map of the Maya area
□ □ □ □ Boundaries of the Central
(southern lowland) area.

Illustrations

Initial Series written with full-figure
glyphs. Stela D, Copan   *frontispiece*

Plate 1   Ruling gods and prognostications for
          heliacal risings of Venus   12

Plate 2   Stela F, Quirigua   13

Plate 3   Lintel 41, Yaxchilan   14

Plate 4   Text on narrow front of Lintel 25, Yaxchilan   15

Plate 5   Praise and offerings to the rain gods   16

Plate 6   Part of divinatory almanac for agriculture 17

Plate 7   Part of medical almanac   18

Plate 8   Part of Divinatory almanac   19

Figure 1 Initial Series texts   36

Figure 2 Initial Series and distance numbers   37

Figure 3 Glyph formation   38

Figure 4 Glyph formation continued   41

Figure 5 Glyph formation continued   42

Figure 6 Glyph formation continued   44

Figure 7 The twenty day signs and heads for
          numbers one to thirteen   45

Figure 8 Month signs and Landa's 'alphabet'   46

Cover   A part of Tikal with stelae. *Courtesy of W. R. Coe*

Introduction

The Maya Indians occupied practically all of what is now the Republic of Guatemala as well as all of British Honduras (Belize), narrow strips of Honduras and El Salvador adjacent to Guatemala's eastern frontier, and the Mexican States of Yucatan, Quintana Roo (Territory), Campeche, and much of Tabasco and Chiapas to the north and west of her territory (map). In the fifteen centuries between the death of Christ and the coming of the Spaniards they developed a civilization remarkable for various features, not the least of which was a fairly well developed writing. In that respect the Maya stood alone in the New World, for other peoples of Middle America, such as the Aztec, never carried writing beyond a rudimentary stage, and in South America there were no hieroglyphs.

Whether New World civilizations blossomed without benefit of Old World tillage – the orthodox view – or whether there was contact across the Pacific, as some maintain, it would be very hard to trace any ancestry for Maya writing in the eastern hemisphere. Accordingly, this Maya system affords us an opportunity of studying the lines along which a writing may develop independent of outside stimulus, a situation which it would be hard to parallel in the Old World.

The Maya system comprises approximately 350 main signs, 370 affixes and about 100 portrait glyphs, principally of deities. Omitting the portrait glyphs and deducting for variants and overlapping between main signs and affixes, the total of Maya glyphs might fall to about 650, but those glyphic elements are combined to form far more numerous compounds. It has been said that no pictographic or ideographic script can manage with less than 500 to 600 signs, whereas 100 or less suffice for a syllabary. Maya writing embraces glyphs of various classes.

It is remarkable that so many glyphs remain undeciphered in view of the fact that the language the glyphs express is known and is spoken to this day, allowing for time shifts such as English shows between Chaucer or, in the case of some of the earliest glyphs, Saxon and B.B.C. news bulletins. A partial explanation is that most Maya ritual terms and religious imagery, unrecorded in Maya-Spanish dictionaries, were lost with the disappearance of the Maya hierarchy.

The Plates

Plate 1 *left*

Ruling gods and prognostications for heliacal risings of Venus

The Venus god in middle picture hurls a spear at the god below, a representation of fertility. That is crops will fail. *Codex Dresden*, p. 46.

Plate 2 *right*

Stela F, Quirigua

This stately monument with personages on two faces and hieroglyphic texts on both sides is twenty-four feet high. Erected in A.D. 761. *After A. P. Maudslay.*

Plate 3
Lintel 41, Yaxchilan
The date 7 *Imix* 14 *Zec* corresponds to
May 7, A.D. 755. The text tells of the
exploits of Bird-Jaguar, the personage on
the right. An enlargement of his head is
on page 11. An original sculpture in the
British Museum.

Plate 4
Text on narrow front of lintel 25,
Yaxchilan
This once stood over a doorway of a
temple. It is now in the British Museum.

Plate 5
Praise and offerings to the rain gods
The four chief rain gods, called Chacs,
were set at the four sides or 'corners' of
the world, and each was assigned a
colour corresponding to the direction.
Codex Dresden, pp. 30 middle to 31 middle.

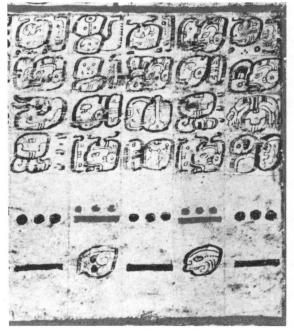

Plate 6
Part of divinatory almanac for agriculture
The first compartment promises good crops; the second, drought; the third, crop failure. *Codex Dresden,* p. 40 middle.

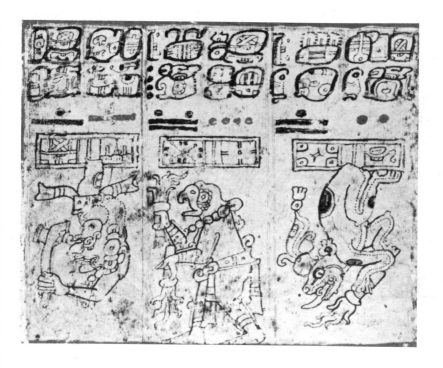

Plate 7
Part of medical almanac
The moon goddess, depicted here, was
patroness of all activities of women and of
diseases and their cure. She was wife of
the sun god, patron of men and their
activities. *Koch*, disease or divine
punishment (the same in Maya eyes), is
illustrated rebus fashion by figures borne
on her shoulders, the Maya term for
which is also *koch*. *Codex Dresden,* p.16
bottom.

Plate 8
Part of divinatory almanac
The moon goddess is again in control
and again rebus writing plays a part.
Cuch, the fate she has in store for mankind,
is illustrated rebus fashion by a load
carried on the back, also *cuch* in Maya.
There is also a play on sounds, *koch* and
cuch. The Maya loved such punning.
Codex Dresden, pp. 19 bottom to 20
bottom.

A brief history of Maya writing

The earliest known hieroglyphs in the New World occur on stone monuments across the Isthmus of Tehuantepec, that narrow belt of land which embraces the south-eastern corner of the Mexican state of Veracruz and immediately adjacent western Tabasco on the Atlantic watershed and eastern Oaxaca with a projection into central Oaxaca, at Monte Albán, on the Pacific side, in actuality somewhat west of the isthmus in a strict geographical sense.

The greatest concentration of these texts is, in fact, at Monte Albán, a ceremonial centre of the Zapotec Indians. Texts are short and in the earliest examples, perhaps of *c.* 500 B.C., largely confined to glyphs of persons and places. On earlier monuments of the Olmec culture certain design elements on clothing, accessories and body may represent embryonic glyphs, but up to the present true hieroglyphs have been found on only one monument from an Olmec ceremonial centre, and that, unfortunately, is not easily dated for it is not in typical early Olmec style. Where and when glyphs to represent the twenty day names first appeared is still not certain, but they are represented in the Monte Albán I period (*c.* 500 B.C.).

On present evidence this incipient writing spread eastward to the Pacific coastal region known as Soconusco, in the State of Chiapas, Mexico, which in the sixteenth century was not Maya-speaking except on the Guatemalan border, and, beyond, to the adjacent Pacific coast and piedmont of Guatemala. There is no evidence as to the language spoken on that coastal strip of Guatemala at that time. Thence use of hieroglyphs, combined with coastal styles in representing the human figure, penetrated to the highlands of Guatemala in the late Formative period, perhaps 200 B.C. At least that is the best reconstruction of events on present evidence. A glyphic text associated with a figure in this late Formative style on a rock at Loltun, in

Yucatan, is the only evidence at present of hieroglyphic writing in the lowlands prior to the birth of Christ.

The glyphs, often badly weathered, on those early monuments, except for those on what is perhaps the latest stela of the series, cannot be assigned to any particular linguistic group. This was the mother script of all systems of writing in Middle America which each culture was to fashion to meet its needs. Minor details suggest local developments even at that early period, and without doubt research will expand them. Growth in most areas was stunted; only the Maya offspring put forth vigorous growth.

Fundamental to all Middle American cultures was the sacred almanac of 260 days, formed by combining a sequence of the numbers 1 to 13 with the twenty day names. By this almanac all activities throughout the area were governed. The general uniformity in the names and glyphs assigned those days throughout Middle America is evidence that all such almanacs, despite differences which have arisen in the course of 2,500 years or more, had a common ancestry. For instance, the fifth and sixth day names in the sequence of twenty were respectively 'snake' and 'death' among the Maya of Yucatan and the Aztec of Mexico City, and in both groups the hieroglyphs for those days are the head of a snake and a skull. Again, the second day is *Ik*, 'wind', or 'breath', in Yucatec Maya and the Tau sign which represents it also means 'life' or 'breath'; in Aztec and related languages that day is called *Eecatl*, a name for the wind god, and the glyph is the head of that god. Naturally, over the centuries divergences arose just as there have been in European day names (e.g. the substitution of Woden's and Thor's days – Wednesday and Thursday – for Latin Mercury and Jupiter days), but the common ancestry of all Middle American calendars is beyond doubt.

There is a little evidence that the highland Maya transmitted their day names to their lowland cousins. The fourteenth Maya day sign is the conventionalized ear of a jaguar, corresponding to the Nahuatl (Aztec and related peoples) day *Ocelotl*, 'Jaguar'. In all Maya calendars, highland and lowland, this day was called *Ix* or *Hix*, a word with no jaguar associations in any lowland Maya language. However, *hix* survives in Kekchi, a north highland Maya tongue, as a term for jaguar, suggesting that Maya day names originated in the Guatemalan highlands or on the Pacific coast.

A deduction may be made as to when the Maya developed their own day names, and the same reasoning supports a highland derivation of those names. In Maya texts the fourth day is designated by the maize symbol, whereas non-Maya calendars picture this day as a lizard or iguana and the Nahuatl people named it *Cuetzpallin*, 'Lizard'. The Yucatec name for this day of maize is *Kan* with variant forms in other lowland calendars, but in Cakchiquel, a highland Maya group, *Kan*, again with the meanings yellow or ripe, has a homonym *Kan*, female iguana. It seems likely that from confusion between those two homonyms arose the shift from Central Mexican lizard to Maya maize.

There is an exception to the Nahuatl use of Lizard for the fourth day: the Nahuatl of Meztitlan in north-eastern Mexico called that day *Xilotl*, 'Green Maize', which immediately reminds us of the Maya maize sign. It is highly unlikely that that is coincidence. The Nahuatl of Meztitlan, probably late comers to the region, were neighbours of the Huaxtec, a Maya group long separated from the Maya homeland by a great distance. As the Nahuatl of Meztitlan show Huaxtec features in their religion, it is reasonable to conjecture that they took over from the Huaxtec also the latter's name for the fourth day. Unfortunately, no list of Huaxtec day names survives. Accepting the surmise, we must conclude that the Maya had their day names before the Huaxtec were separated from the main body of Maya. As the Huaxtec were closer to lowland Maya languages than to highland Maya, could we date that separation, we would have a *terminus ante quem* for lowland Maya use of day names. According to the Swadesh theory for dating the separation of languages, called glottochronology, which however, is discredited in the eyes of many linguists, that separation took place about 500 B.C. Although the accuracy of Swadesh's method is highly questionable, it does serve as a rough and ready guide to when two linguistic groups separated. Moreover, it does find some support in archaeology in this particular case, so perhaps we can hazard that the lowland Maya had their twenty day names by about 500 B.C.; and, because of the overwhelming importance among them of the days in divination for every aspect of daily life, it is reasonable to suppose that by then or not long after, the lowland Maya had the corresponding glyphs.

However, the earliest surviving text of definitely Maya character is considerably later; it is at the large highland site of Kaminaljuyu, and is datable around 200–100 B.C. on stylistic grounds. Despite their lead in early texts, the highland Maya appear to have lost interest in the subject, for no inscriptions of the Classic or later periods have been recovered in their territory. In contrast, it was in the lowlands, embracing the whole peninsula of Yucatan and the broad strip at its base, bisected by the River Usumacinta, flowing north-westward into the Gulf of Mexico, and the Sarstoon river with easterly course to the Bay of Honduras, that the great development of Maya writing took place.

The earliest firmly dated monument in the lowlands is at Tikal, greatest of Maya ceremonial centres, and carries a calendric text corresponding to A.D. 292 (European equivalents of Maya dates are according to the Goodman-Martínez-Thompson correlation, accepted by nearly all Maya students). This date is expressed in the highly complex Initial Series system, a vigesimal count of multiples of the *tun* (year of 360 days) reckoned, as were practically all Maya dates, from a mythical starting point corresponding to 3113 B.C., long before the Maya calendar was invented.

This elaborate system of dating or something close to it first appears in southern Veracruz, western Chiapas and on the Pacific coast of Guatemala, but later was used only by the lowland Maya who recorded countless dates in it on stone, pottery, murals, and their paper of bark cloth. The Maya had the (for us) unfortunate habit of destroying or discarding their stone monuments, so it is virtually certain that earlier stelae once existed. Indeed, this earliest stela had been smashed; the recovered piece had been used in construction fill.

It is a reasonable inference that during the Classic period the southern lowlanders spoke a language ancestral to the closely related Chol, Putun and Chorti Maya languages or dialects current there in the sixteenth century; in Yucatan the speech was surely Yucatec Maya which even today is not far separated lexically from the above Choloid group (Tikal probably lay near the boundary between the Chol languages and Yucatec). The relationship was closer than that of Spanish and Italian, but somewhat more distant than that between Spanish and Portuguese. Two millennia ago differences must have been considerably less marked.

Recording of texts on monuments almost ceased with the end of the Classic period (*c.* A.D. 900), but three hieroglyphic books of later date have survived. These are composed of long strips of bark paper, with polished surfaces of lime and size, written on both sides. The strips are folded like a screen and pull out for reading, each fold forming a page (Pls. 5–8). They are named *Codices Dresden*, *Madrid*, and *Paris* from the cities which now shelter them. As aids to decipherment these books, particularly *Codex Dresden*, the best written, have several advantages over texts of the Classic period:

1. They are nearer present-day speech by several centuries, for they were composed A.D. 1300–1500, and contain glyphs, simple and compound, not found on the earlier monuments, and there is evidence that a number of these were developed in the post-Classic period. Roughly, codex texts are to sixteenth-century Maya as Chaucer is to modern English, whereas those of the Classic period would bear the relationship Bede has to our speech.

2. Apart from the time factor in language change, most Classic-period texts of the southern lowlands were inscribed by Maya almost certainly of the Choloid group of languages, but vocabularies and grammars in those languages and dialects are inadequate and none of value of the sixteenth or seventeenth century exists. In fact two of the tongues are extinct. On the other hand, there is excellent lexical and grammatical material for Yucatec from the sixteenth century on, and there is good evidence that all three books were written by Yucatec Maya. Their language is widely spoken to this day in Yucatan, Campeche, Quintana Roo and British Honduras, but the old ritualistic and ceremonial terms were not recorded by the Franciscan composers of dictionaries, and passed into oblivion early in the colonial period.

3. The texts in the codices are profusely supplemented by illustrations which, standing below the passages to which they refer, are extremely useful in identifying the subject under discussion. Matters such as divination for hunting, beekeeping, sowing, weather, disease, new-year ceremonies as well as divination connected with heliacal risings of Venus and days on which solar eclipses might be

expected have been identified in that way, and have yielded many decipherments. These include names of gods and glyphs for colours, directions, sky, earth, drought, rainy skies, maize, cacao, animals, diseases, death, misfortune and good tidings in addition to some prepositions and verbal stems. Progress continues along those lines. On the monuments, apart from successes in calendrical matters, a subject to which the Maya of the Classic period devoted much space, progress has been much slower. Those texts do not deal with divination for everyday life, the only illustration is often a chief impersonating a god in a static pose, and, as we have seen, there is more difficulty with the language.

The formation of Maya hieroglyphs

Areas for texts are divided into approximately square glyph blocks narrowly separated one from another by grooves on stone monuments, by plain borders in the books. On stelae, these blocks are usually arranged in vertical columns, for convenience lettered A, B, C, D, etc. from left to right and numbered 1, 2, 3, 4, etc. vertically. Blocks are read in pairs starting with A1 (top left corner), then to B1 (top of adjacent column), then back to A2 in column 1, B2, A3, B3, etc. From the bottom of the first pair of columns, the reader then passes to the top of the adjacent pair of columns (C1, D1), and then downward again in pairs (Fig. 2). An inscription may be horizontal; if glyphs are in a single line, they are read from left to right; if the horizontal text is in two lines (Pl. 4), the arrangement conforms to that of vertical masses: the glyphs are read in blocks of four (A1, B1, A2, B2, C1, D1, C2, D2, etc.).

Divinatory almanacs which fill the greater part of the books are divided into compartments, *t'ol*, usually of four glyph blocks read also in pairs top to bottom, an explanatory illustration below and in the middle an abbreviated record of the distance forward from the previous *t'ol* and the days reached (Pl. 5–8).

To fit a long text into limited space, glyph blocks could be halved, usually by a vertical, but sometimes a horizontal, line, or the glyph block could be quartered, allowing two or four glyphs or glyph compounds to occupy the normal space for one. Halving and quartering is often confined to the second half of a text, as though the artist realized he was running short of space. As glyphs had to conform to available space, the height of each glyph in a vertically divided block was about twice its width; an opposite distortion occurred if the division was horizontal.

Shortage of space was also overcome by reducing the size of glyph blocks in subsidiary areas.

A Maya glyph may stand by itself, but commonly smaller elements, called affixes, are attached. These can stand above or to left of the main sign (prefixes) or to right or below (postfixes). A main sign with affixes or combined with another main sign with or without additional affixes, is a glyph compound. A prefix can be either to left or above and a postfix in either of its two positions without altering the meaning of the compound (Fig. 3 a–c). Choice of position was largely governed by available space and a desire to minimize distortion of the main sign. In practice some prefixes almost always stood above and some postfixes below, but that probably was a matter of habit. As order of reading was prefix, main sign, postfix, exchange of prefix and postfix was not permissible, but that rule seems in rare cases not to have been observed. Similarly, the Aztec in their writing sometimes broke that rule. For example, Mixcoatl, Cloud Serpent, is found with the *coatl* sign above that corresponding to *mix*. This is evidence that the compound was seen as a whole, not read particle by particle.

Unusual elongation of the affix resulting from limited space was partly remedied in two ways: the edge adjoining the main sign was suppressed, care being taken that no essential detail was on the suppressed part, and in such cases the main sign appears to overlap the affix (Fig. 3 g); alternatively, symmetry was retained by doubling the affix, an arrangement which did not affect the meaning (Fig. 3 d, e).

Nearly always the base of the affix adjoins the main sign so that in effect the affix rotates around the main sign. To left of the main sign an affix is on its side with base to observer's right; to right it is on its side with base to observer's left; below, it is upside down.

There is fluidity in Maya writing, for instance affixes sometimes become main elements and *vice versa* for calligraphic reasons without any change of meaning (Fig. 3 *f*, *g*). Sometimes, an affix perhaps representing a preposition is promoted to main sign when it represents a homonymous noun (*tan*, toward and time). There may be no true main sign, the compound consisting of an affix, often doubled, to which other affixes are attached (Fig. 3 *h*, *i*). Sometimes doubling is to overcome the awkward fitting of an elongated affix into the square space assigned the main sign; at other times it is a phonetic device to represent a repeated speech particle (Fig. 3 *i*).

Angularity has no place in standard Maya writing; corners of main signs and affixes are gently rounded. A few glyphs do not conform to this square or rectangular form with rounded corners. Those are portrait glyphs, for the most part of gods, animals, birds and so on, as well as representations of hearts (symbol of human sacrifice), hands, crossed legs, bones, axes, merchants' packs, etc. Naturally, writing on paper is more cursive than on stone.

Two or more main elements often with affixes added may occupy a single glyph block. This may be because they are to be read together to form a single word. A good example of this process is the *kintunyaabil*, drought, glyph (Fig. 3 *l*) which combines the main signs corresponding to *kin*, *tun*, *haab* (*yaab* – *h* changes to *y* to indicate relationship) and the relationship affix *il*. Two sequent main elements in a text, particularly if related in subject matter, may occupy a single glyph block (Fig. 5 *d*), but if available space was longer than required, a compound could be expanded to fill two glyph blocks (Fig. 5 *e*,*f*).

On present evidence main signs tend to embrace nouns and verbal stems; affixes to represent adjectives (black, green, Fig. 3 *a*–*c*, *u*, malevolent, Fig. 5 *c*, *d*); prepositions (to, in, on, Fig. 3 *k*); adverbs (backward, Fig. 6 *g*, *h*); qualifying terms (woe to, Fig. 6 *n*, *o*, lord of, Fig. 6 *d*–*f*, heart of, Fig. 3 *j*); verbal suffixes (*bil*, Fig. 5 *q*, *s*); distinguishing attributes (Bacabs, Fig. 4 *a, c'*); relationship (*il,* Fig. 4 *n, o, al,* Fig. 3 *j*). A few nouns are affixes presumably because of their elongated shapes (wood and flint point, Fig. 3 *u, z*).

Expectedly, there is some variation between carved signs of the Classic period and painted (written) reproductions of the same elements in the later hieroglyphic books, but such differences are minor and for the most part arose from the development of cursive writing on paper rather than from the passage of time. Compare, for instance carved and painted day and month signs (Figs. 7, 8) or representations of the *yax,* green, prefix (Figs. 2, B7, F2, 4 *y* contrasted with Fig. 4 *g*) or the *u* prefix (Fig 2, F10 contrasted with Fig. 5 *q*).

Landa's alphabet and the task of decipherment

The history of the decipherment of Maya hieroglyphs opens with Diego de Landa, a Franciscan who reached Yucatan in 1549 when the Spaniards had hardly completed the pacification of the country. Landa, intelligent and with an interest in native culture all too rare in the sixteenth century, was Provincial Vicar of Yucatan and later its bishop. He began collecting information on Maya religion, history, customs and everyday life which he embodied in a lengthy manuscript, *Relación de las cosas de Yucatán*. The original was lost, but a version, perhaps abbreviated, was found and published just over a century ago.

Landa gave detailed information on the complex Maya calendar together with drawings of the twenty sequent day signs and of the eighteen (20-day) months. Those drawings identified as Maya the many inscriptions on stone – stairways, cornices, lintels, panels, altars and, above all, stelae – which are so prominent in Maya ceremonial centres (loosely called cities) scattered over the Maya lowlands. Such sites have been found in large numbers during the past 125 years, and, indeed, continue to be found beneath the dense rain forest to this day.

Landa, describing briefly Maya writing, claimed that it was alphabetic. In support he wrote a three-word sentence (but the arrangement of the glyphs was European, not Maya) and gave glyphs purportedly corresponding to each letter of the Spanish alphabet (except *d, f, g, r* and *v*, not found in Yucatec) as well as sounds not in Spanish (glottalized *k, p,* and *t*), but he omitted from his 'alphabet' glyphs for *ch, ch', tz* and *dz'*, all very common Maya sounds. Students of a century ago applied Landa's key to the decipherment of Maya texts in the books with enthusiasm but without any success (Fig. 8).

In fact, the evidence is incontrovertible that Landa gave, not the *sounds* of the ABC, but the *names* of the letters, asking his Maya informant for the Maya equivalents. The latter responded wirh signs as close as he could get to the Spanish names. Thus for *a*, *b*, *c*, pronounced *ah*, *bay*, *say*, he drew the head of a turtle, *ac* in Maya; a foot, Maya symbol for travel and roads, *be* (pronounced *bay*); and a truncated form of the month sign *Zec* (pronounced *sek*). Unfortunately, feet are extremely scarce in Maya texts, and turtle heads and the month sign *Zec* are not common. Similarly for *x*, pronounced *xay*, an exceedingly common sound in Maya, Landa's informant drew the head of a vomiting man; *xe* (*xay*) is vomit in Maya, but vomiting men do not figure in Maya texts. Again, for *u* the informant gave a sign like a query mark, but which represents in Maya a lock of hair. That is the identifying sign of women in general and the moon goddess in particular. *U* in Yucatec means moon. When there was a glyphic element corresponding to a sound supplied by Landa, the informant drew it, for example, he gave the sign for god, *ku*, for Landa's *cu* (Landa, who had a poor ear for sounds, failed to distinguish between hard *c* and its glottalized form, written *k* in Maya), and he drew the locative sign for *ti*, a correct correspondence in sound. A handful of glyphs, mainly day signs, also in Landa's book, occur in *The Books of Chilam Balam*, written by Maya in Spanish script during the colonial period.

Following failure to read the texts with Landa's alphabet, research turned to other approaches. Name glyphs of gods were identified by their positions above portraits, and from Landa's information it was possible to identify directional and colour glyphs. In quick succession the many signs associated with the immensely complicated Maya calendar were isolated and their values proved arithmetically. By about 1930 that seam was largely worked out.

The linguist Whorf (1933) revived the view that Maya glyphs were phonetic; he believed that each glyphic element represented consonant plus vowel or *vice versa*, and that usually these stood for the root of a verb. He failed to prove his case, and his views were not endorsed by any other student of the subject. In 1952 a young Russian, Yuri Knorozov, to the accompaniment of much publicity announced that with a Marxist-Leninist approach he had found the key to Maya writing. He maintained that many of the signs represented consonant plus vowel or vowel plus consonant, but as Maya words tend to be monosyllabic, the second sign of a compound was to be read as the consonant only. As an illustration of his approach we may note an example which he himself has cited as confirmation of the success of his approach. The long recognized glyph for dog is composed of two elements (Fig. 3 *n*). To the first he assigns the sound *tzu*, the second (the sacrifice symbol) he identifies as Landa's *l* (pronounced *ele*) in Spanish. Apparently not accepting that Landa gave the names of the alphabet, not the sounds, he identifies this *l* glyph as representing a certain freshwater fish called *lu* in Yucatec. The combination then reads *tzulu* to give *tzul*, dog. The common Maya names for dog are *pek* in Yucatec and *tz'i* in practically all other Maya languages. *Tzul* was almost certainly not a pre-Columbian term for dog, but was introduced after the Spanish conquest to designate the new breeds introduced by the Spaniards. It occurs in no Maya document and only in two late Spanish-Maya dictionaries, where the word is given with the meaning of domestic dog and is contrasted with the name for the native dog. The word is quite unknown today. Knorozov allows himself great latitude on sound values, thus one sign can stand for *om*, *an*, and *hun*; another for *mal*, *nal*, and *mol*; a third for *kin* and *cun*, and he ignores glottal stops, for a sign covers *pidz'*, *p'iz* and *pedz'*, although we know the Maya very carefully distinguished glottalized from non-glottalized sounds. That is playing poker with deuces wild. With this key decipherment should have been rapid, but in recent years no phonetic decipherments have followed. An attempt to read Maya texts according to the Knorozov system with the aid of a computer at the research centre in Novosibirsk was equally unsuccessful; the results were condemned by Knorozov himself. That many affixes serve only as prefixes and others only as postfixes also argues against the thesis.

Overmuch space has been assigned to this 'system' because it has attracted amateurs and a sprinkling of linguists with little or no knowledge of Maya hieroglyphs; keys to codes and simple explanations of complex matters have strange powers to allure. I know of only one serious student of the subject who supports the Knorozov system, and he with reservations.

'Rules' of glyphic composition

Publication of catalogues of Maya glyphs (Zimmermann, 1956, and Thompson, 1962), by making material freely available, produced a flood of 'decipherments' from persons anxious to try their hands at the game of reading an unknown script but who had little or no background knowledge of the field. Almost without exception such readings are worthless because they fail to conform to what can be deduced as to the nature of glyphic composition.

The most important of those 'rules', as I see them, are as follows:

1. Maya glyphic elements certainly stand for nouns, adjectives, verbal stems, prepositions, and speech particles, but as Maya is largely a monosyllabic language, such glyphs generally represent monosyllables. Compound words, formed by joining two nouns or an adjective or a speech particle to a noun or verbal stem are represented by compound glyphs. For example, *Yaxkin*, name of the sixth 20-day month, is the adjective *yax*, green, new or strong, qualifying *kin*, sun or day. It refers to the strong suns of the dry season. The glyph, corresponding to the speech, comprises an adjectival prefix (*yax*) attached to a main sign, *kin*, sun or day. The *kin* sign, in turn, usually has a 'cords' postfix, referring to the sun's rays (Fig. 8; p. 64). Again, *ku*, god, becomes the term for goddess by prefixing the female indicator *x* (pronounced *sh*). The Spaniards, having difficulty in mouthing *x* before a consonant, usually rendered and wrote it *ix*. The *cauac* glyph, usually associated with rain storms, also stands for *ku*, god. Glyphically, the head of a woman represents the female gender. Accordingly, woman's head prefixed to *cauac* stood for *xku* or *ixku*, goddess (Fig. 3 *p*).

Again the relationship suffix *il*, added to *tun* (360-day year), forms *tunil*, year of, and the suffixing of *al* to *caan*, sky, becomes *caanal*, on high. Both are written as compounds with main sign and postfix, corresponding to the spoken words (Fig.3 *m*, *q*). Attention has already

Figure 1
Initial series texts
Left: Text with numerical bars and dots
and symbolic forms of period glyphs.
Temple 18, Palenque. *After A. Ruz*

with minor additions.
Right: Text with head forms for both
numbers and periods. Stela F, Quirigua.
After A. P. Maudslay.

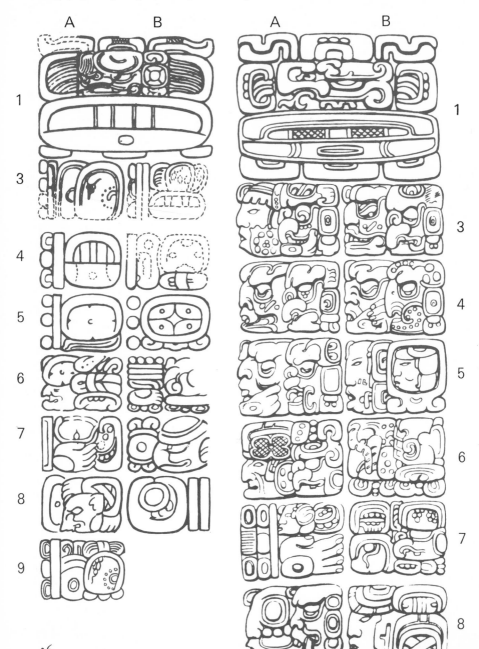

Figure 2
Initial series and distance numbers
Inscription on the back of Stela 3,
Piedras Negras with Initial Series and four

other dates connected by distance
numbers. The hollow space is occupied
by the head of a ruler. *After A. P.
Maudslay.*

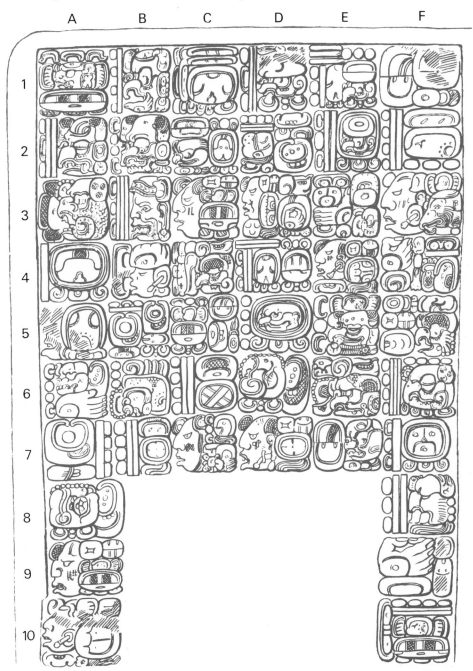

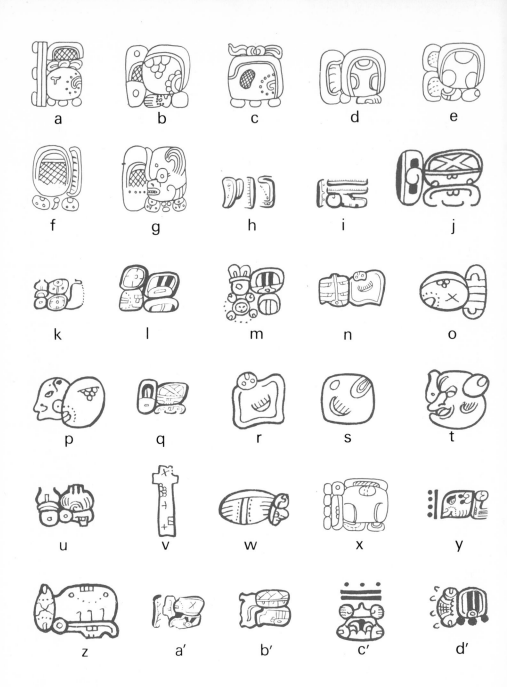

a

b

c

d

e

f

g

h

i

j

k

l

m

n

o

p

q

r

s

t

u

v

w

x

y

z

a'

b'

c'

d'

Figure 3
Glyph formation

a–c: month *Ch'en* with black affix to left,
above and infixed. *d–e:* month *Zec* with
comb affix single and double. *f–g:* comb
affix (*f*) becomes personified fish deity
as main sign (*g*). *h:* three affixes – *baat ca
kal* – form verb without main sign.
i: u cacabil, cacao glyph, formed of
affixes only. *j: yol*, the heart of, *caanal*, the
sky, literally, on high. *k: ti likin*, in the
east, literally at sun rise. *l: kintun-yaabil*,
drought, literally, *haab* (year) of excessive
sun. *m: tun* (year) of war (shield) and
terror (*zac*, white, used for its homonym
terror). *n: pek*, dog, incorporating heart
glyph. *o: cauac* as *ku*, god, with
reverential postfix (*tzil?*). *p: cauac* as *ku*,
god, with female head prefixed, *xku*,
goddess. *q: ek caanal*, black on high.
r–s: heart as sacrificial glyph; *t:* bat as
blood drinker with heart details infixed.
u: ti yaxche, at the ceiba, literally, green
tree. *v: kuche*, divine tree, cedar (*cauac-ku*
with *che* outline). *w: kakche*, ebony,
literally fire tree. *x: 4 te Zec. y:* god
Bolonyocte. *z:* stone and wood club
affixes signifying strife with *bak*, terror.
a': cuch with *te* determinative. *b': cuch*
with mat determinative. *c': mac*, turtle
carapace, representing month (13) *Mac*.
d': coc, turtle, qualifying *tun*, year as one of
misery (*coc*).

Figure 4
Glyph formation continued
a: turtle Bacab. *b:* milpa. *c:* milpa with
suffix infixed in *cab. d:* inverted bat head
8 *katuns. e:* maize growing from seed
(*ixim*). *f:* new maize (*nal*). *g:* new green
maize. *h:* red maize (doubling indicates
much?). *i–j:* maize gruel (*zaca*). *k:* round
maize cakes (*pec uah*). *l:* maize steeped in
lime (*tan*). *m:* abundance of maize (*kan-
imix*). *n:* offering of new maize (*holil
nal*). *o:* a year of green maize (*tunil yax
nal*). *p: hanal*, eating, eatables. *q: can
chibal*, fierce devourer (here death).
r: west. *s:* maker of life, Chacs' titular
glyph. *t:* Chac, maker of life, god. *u: u
dz'abil*, his given. *v: cuch ca kal*, carried on
back. *w:* fertility aspect of Itzam Na with
maize growing from hole in forehead.
x: hun hatzcab, one dawn. *y:* new (*yax*)
dawn. *z:* new dawn. Head of god nine
with *yax* attribute substitutes for *yax*,
new. *a':* the four Bacabs, the four gods.
b': conch Bacab. *c':* Bacab festival (*kin*).
d': Chac zacal men, the red weaving
craftswoman, the old red goddess. *e':* red
goddess of spinning and weaving.

a   b   c   d   e

f   g   h   i   j   k

l   m   n   o   p

q   r   s   t   u

v   w   x   y   z

a′   b′   c′   d′   e′

a   b   c   d

e   f   g   h

i   j   k   l

m   n   o   p

q   r   s

t   u   v   w   x

Figure 5
Glyph formation continued
a : the old goddess the weaving craftswoman. *b : ah men*, craftsman, title of
several deities. *c :* evil prefix over *men*,
doer; malevolent. *d :* evil fierce sun, *lob?*
kintun. e–f : kintun occupying two blocks
with evil prefix over both parts. *g :* pack,
merchant gods' attribute. *h : bolon (h)ol*,
uncontaminated offering (of) *balche; cab*,
honey, beneath specifies *balche* here is
mead. *i : bak*, flesh, with offering suffix,
(right) warns *balche* sign (left) here means
game. *j :* sacrifice of meat. *k :* war terror;
jaguar paw, *chacmol*, prefix is war symbol,
with *bak*, flesh, but here its homonym
terror. *l :* eight with maize affixes, symbol
of maize god and maize. *m :* jaguar ear,
symbol of night sun. *n :* jaguar ear
representing day *Ocelotl*, jaguar, in
Mexican codex. *o :* same representing
equivalent Maya day *Ix*. *p :* Four deer on
high; deer hoof represents whole deer.
q : u kochbil, his borne on shoulders, *bil*
participial suffix. *r : u tanlah nal*, his
offering of new maize, *bil*, attached to
maize, here indicating fresh. *s : tanlahbil*,
offered, with *bil* participial postfix;
maize sign with lunar action postfix, *kal*,
probably indicating ripened. *t : Imix*-
comb-*Imix* compound. *u :* same with fish
substituted for comb affix. *v :* count back
to compound with vulture head
substituting for locative *ti*, to, because it
normally has this sign on forehead. In
the Palencano-Chol language *ta*
corresponds to *ti*, but also means
excrement. Excrement head, descriptive
of its habits, is the Palencano-Chol name
for vulture. *w : hel*, change, glyph with
hidẓ' expiration, prefix. *x :* same with
death affix replacing expiration.

Figure 6 *below*
Glyph formation continued
a: *haab, cauac* sign with cords suffixed.
b: seating of *haab* compound. *c*: same
with seating prefix infixed in *haab*.
d: Kinich Ahau, Lord owner of sun.
e: Lord owner of jaguar skin. *f*: Lord
owner of divine bat, *halach?*, ruler of
Copan. *g*: *xoc*, count, with water
substituting for *xoc*, shark, to backward.
h: same but *xoc*, shark, used for *xoc*
count. *i*: worm or snake prefixed to 13
Ahau to indicate starting point of a count
back. *j*: *u kaz*, its evil, augural glyph.
k: death, augural glyph. *l*: *u koch*, his
disease or divine punishment, augural
glyph. *m*: disease or punishment of the
maize god. *n*: woe to, *numya*, mankind.
o: woe and misery, *numya pop*, to the seed.
p: halfway, *kaz*, good tidings. *q*: rainy
sky. Rain drops affixed to sky sign.

Figure 7 *right*
**The twenty day signs and heads for
numbers 1 to 13**
As in all illustrations, glyphs with heavy
outline are copied from painted signs in
the codices; those with thin outline are
from sculptured monuments.

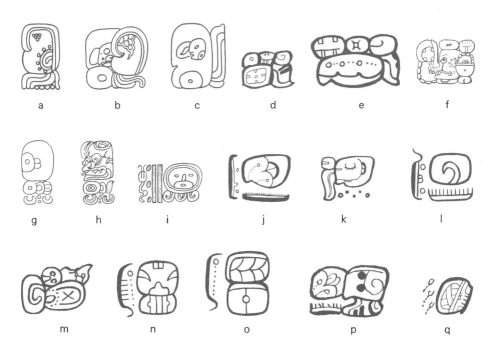

a   b   c   d   e   f

g   h   i   j   k   l

m   n   o   p   q

Imix

  Ik Akbal Kan Chicchan

 Chicchan Cimi   Manik Lamat

 Lamat Muluc   Oc Chuen

 Chuen Eb Ben Ix

 Men Cib Caban

Edz'nab Cauac Ahau

 1   2   3   4   5   6

 7   8   9   10   11   12   13

45

Pop	Uo	Zip	Zotz'		Zec
Zec	Xul	Yaxkin	Mol	Ch'en	Yax
Zac	Ceh	Mac		Kankin	
Muan	Pax	Kayab		Cumku	Uayeb

A	A	A	B	B	C	T	E	H
I	CA	K	L	L	M	N	O	O
PP	CU	KU	X	X	U	U	Z	P

Figure 8
Month signs and Landa's 'alphabet'
Above are examples of the eighteen
'months' of twenty days each, together
with the glyph of the five fateful days at
the end of the year called *Uayeb*. Below,
the glyphs correspond to the Spanish
names – not the sounds – of the
alphabet according to Bishop Diego de
Landa.

been drawn to the compound *kintunyaabil*, drought, composed of
three monosyllabic nouns and a monosyllabic speech particle *il*
(Fig. 3 *l*).

On the other hand, compound terms not formed by combining
various independent words or which, if thus originally formed, had
ceased to be recognized as such, were not, on present evidence,
represented glyphically in a true syllabic manner. For instance, the
compound *puczikal*, heart, is represented by a conventionalized
portrait of that organ which still retains the shape of the heart com-
plete with formalized but recognizable aorta (Fig. 3 *r*, *s*). It was not
expressed as a compound of signs for *puuc*, range of hills, and *zical*,
flat board for copal nodules. Still less would it have been written in
the Knorozov syllabic system with signs for *pu*, *cu*, *zi*, *ki* and *al*,
assuming that glyphs for all of those existed. There is no cause to
suppose that a final consonant could be lopped off a monosyllabic
word: *yax* could not serve for *ya*, *lu* or *le* for *l*, or *kan* for *ka*, etc.

Again there is no evidence that glyphic elements could be combined haphazard to form new words. To illustrate, *te* (also *che* because
there was a sound shift from *t* to *ch*) signifies, among other things,
wood, and its glyph appears in many homonyms (Fig. 3 *u–y*), but the
te sign could not be combined with the glyph for *tan* or *taan* to read
tetaan, chosen, because *te* does not enter into the composition of the
word, which is the verbal stem *tet* with the participial suffix *aan* added.
Similarly, *te* and *ex*, loin cloth, could not be combined to form *teex*,
you; they are no more separable elements of *teex* than *as* is of waste
or asked.

In short: a glyphic element representing a definite sound or object
or idea does not change those values when joined to others in a
compound glyph.

2. The Maya made great use of homonyms (words with the same

sound but different meanings) as in rebus writing, for instance, children's drawings of an eye, a tin can and waves, standing for sea, to read 'I can see', or as in heraldry – the famous double rebus of Abbot Islip which comprises a picture of the abbot slipping reinforced by an eye and a plant slip, or that of Walter Lyhart showing a hart lying in water.

The glyph for *te* or *che*, wood, mentioned above, supplies good examples of rebus writing, for it is used to express various homonyms.

With the meaning tree, it is attached to the glyph *yax*, green, new or strong, to give *yaxche* or *yaxte* (the first current in Yucatec, the second in Choloid languages), the green tree, name for the sacred ceiba (*Bombax pentandra*); outlining a tree trunk with inset *cauac* (*ku*, divine) symbols, it represents *kuche*, divine tree, the Spanish cedar, so called because it alone was used in making wooden idols and other religious paraphernalia; joined to the *kak*, fire, sign, it denotes *kakche*, the ebony tree (Fig. 3 *u–w*).

The English language has a few collective terms used in counting certain objects: loaves of bread, slices of cake, head of cattle are examples. Maya employed great numbers of these numerical classifiers. Among them is *te*, used for counting *inter alia* days, months and years. In writing, these were often omitted, presumably to save space, but sometimes they are given. Examples are: *ca te tunob*, 2 tuns (years); *can te Zec*, day 4 of the 'month' *Zec* (Fig. 3 *x*). The wood sign serves rebus fashion for the homonymous *te* numerical classifier.

Bolonyocte, whose name probably means something like Nine Strides or Innumerable Strides, was an important Maya god, almost certainly a god of merchants. *Bolon*, nine, has the secondary meanings of innumerable and uncontaminated. His glyph consists of the number nine prefixed to the head of an animal which represents the day *Oc*, and the *te* sign is postfixed, again used rebus fashion (Fig. 3 *y*).

The affixes of wood (*te*) and flint knife (by extension, stone) occur together as affixes of two glyphs of an augural nature. With great acumen the German epigrapher Barthel (1955) matched these with a Yucatec Maya expression *che* (*etel*) *tunich*, cudgels (and) stones, a metaphor for strife. *Naczah che okol, naczah tunich okol*, lift up cudgels, lift up stones, is to rebel. One of the main signs with which these occur (Cat. No. 558) I have read as *bak*, meat, but with a homonym *bak*, terror. The whole then would read 'Terror of strife (cudgels and stones)'. Here, then, *te* is used in a metaphorical sense (Fig. 3 *z*).

Te was also employed as a determinative, that is to say it specified a particular meaning for the glyph to which it was attached. *Cuch*, burden carried on the back, has secondary meanings much employed in the hieroglyphic books. Most important of these is fate or destiny, used particularly in recording the fate which the incoming year held for mankind or the fateful influence that a deity wielded on days when he was in power. In that sense death is the *cuch* of a particular incoming year or, in almanacs treating of disease, disease of the pox group (*kaak*, fire, here used rebus fashion), is the divine *cuch* of (that is sent by) the moon goddess on the days in question (Pl. 8). *Cuch* can also mean seat of authority, a ruler's throne. To differentiate, *cuch* when used as burden (fate) usually has the *te* sign added; when referring to the ruler's seat, the mat symbol is added because mat was a metaphor for authority (Fig. 3 *a'*, *b'*). *Te* is added probably because the carrying frame used to this day by highland Maya and in Central Mexico is of wood. Present day Yucatec Maya use sacks or net bags, and illustrations in the codices show a sort of supporting pad, but it is reasonable to suppose that the carrying frame was in use in ancient times when long-distance trading was common. The mat sign, like the wood symbol, was a determinative, indicating the sense in which *cuch* was to be read. Many other instances of use of glyphs to represent homonyms appear in subsequent pages. Among them may be noted *kaz*, evil and halfway; *kak*, fire and pox; and *zac*, white, weave and fear.

The Maya very carefully differentiated in their speech between simple and fortis consonants, of which there are five pairs in Yucatec, written respectively as *c* and *k*, *ch* and *ch'*, *p* and *p'* (often written *pp* in early sources), *tz* and *dz'* (written as a reversed *c* in early and some modern texts), and *t* and *t'* (*th* in early sources). The Maya would no more say *pat*, 'to model clay', when he meant *p'at*, 'to leave someone', than we would say *pat* when we meant *bat*.

The Maya use of rebus writing probably derives from their love of punning. In a Maya colonial document (Roys, 1933, pp. 70–73) there is an account of a migration in which are listed the many settlements through which the invaders passed. In nearly every case there is a pun on the place name. For instance, they came to P'oole where they increased in numbers (*p'olhob*); at Ticooh, 'place of the *coh*, puma', they haggled for what was expensive (*coohi*). In the list there are thirty-four place names with attached puns containing one of the above consonants which can be simple or fortis. In every case a fortis in the place name is followed by a fortis in the pun and the same is true of the simple consonants. The Maya book of medical incantations known as *Ritual of the Bacabs* (Roys, 1965) is full of similar puns and again the rule is to match fortis with fortis and simple with simple consonant. I have not examined every example, but exceptions do not exist or are very rare.

One is confident that that care in punning in speech was matched in writing, particularly as failure to match the consonants might produce ambiguities in short glyphic texts (in divinatory passages they seldom exceed four glyph blocks). Furthermore, no cases of identified glyphs being used in that loose way have been found;

cuch never stands for *kuch*, vulture or its homonym thread, nor *kab*, hand, for *cab*, earth or honey. If one ignores these clear restrictions, it is easy with a largely monosyllabic language to produce 'readings', but they are not worth the paper they are written on. Unfortunately, there has been a heavy crop of such decipherments.

3. Certain glyphs can have different phonetic values when they correspond to synonyms in spoken Maya. A turtle carapace, a term for which is *mac* in Yucatec, often appears as the main element of the month sign *Mac* (Fig. 3 *c'*), but *coc* is the name of a variety of turtle. In a few cases a turtle carapace is attached to the tun, year, and once to the new maize glyph, and as *coc* can also mean mean or miserable, Barthel has suggested that in those places it qualifies the year (Fig. 3 *d'*) as miserable; read as *mac* it makes no sense. Turtle carapace can also serve as an attributive. Surmounted by the insignia of the Bacabs affix, it is the name glyph of the Bacab who is clad in a turtle carapace and whose name is perhaps Ah yax ac, Lord Green Turtle (Fig. 4 *a*).

4. Ideograms, that is to say glyphs which stand for an object, but not for its sound, are common. The compound for milpa (corn field) supplies a good example. This consists of the glyphs for seed and earth (*cab*) alongside each other or one above the other. Both normally have postfixes, but both can be omitted (Fig. 4 *b, c*). The combination expresses the idea, not the sound. The heart sign stands for human sacrifice because the commonest form of that rite was by removal of the heart (Fig. 3 *r, s*). Alternatively, this idea could be expressed by placing the head of a bat alongside the heart or the bat may appear alone but with details of the heart glyph infixed (Fig. 3 *t*). The reason for this combination is that the vampire bat, so common in the Maya lowlands, draws blood from its victims and is thus an excellent symbol for sacrifice.

Kan, which is the sign for the fourth day and which seemingly once stood for ripe and yellow, is a general sign for maize. With varying affixes and attached main signs it stands for the seed, the young plant, new corn, growing or on the cob (called *elote* in Mexico), the maize gruel called *zaca*, and dishes of maize or maize and meat such as venison, turkey (tamales or stews). It is as though we had a general sign for pig and expressed pork, bacon, chitterlings and pig's trotters by adding symbols (Fig. 4 *e–n*). All Maya groups used distinctive names for all stages of maize from seedling to cooking pot or grill; it was and is their daily bread. Indeed, it has been calculated that in some Maya groups, even at the present time, 80 per cent of the individual's food consumption is maize. Thus the *kan* sign represents the object, not its sound. *Kan* and the day sign *Imix* with certain affixes form a compound which stands for something like abundance (Fig. 4 *m*), but it is difficult to determine meanings of glyphs such as *Imix* which go back to the beginnings of Maya writing and the names of which probably were current long before that; many religious associations have clustered around them in the intervening centuries. *Imix* embodies such conceptions as earth, water and abundance which in Maya thought were related (the earth was the back of a crocodile afloat in a great lake). Accordingly, the precise meaning of this compound will never be known with certitude.

5. Pictograms may also serve as ideograms; the heart as a symbol for human sacrifice has been noted. This is a pictogram, for its outline is not that of a normal glyph, but is heart-shaped, and the element at top seems to depict the aorta (Fig. 3 *r, s*).

Again, certain heads with prominent teeth in upper jaw but no lower jaw display a pair of antennae-like objects rising from the crown, such as some bee gods have (Fig. 4 *p*). They surely represent food or the act of eating; the Yucatec word *hanal* (root *han*) means both, but *kux*, now to gnaw in Yucatec, was probably the term a millennium ago, for it is the current word for eating (biting) in other lowland Maya tongues. Locusts in Mexican art have straight or curved antennae and frequently have large teeth, surely to mark their eating capabilities, in upper jaw and a vestigial or absent lower jaw. As the locust is the great devourer dreaded throughout Middle America, plausibly this head which stands for eating incorporates characteristics of the locust as its distinctive feature.

The Maya made great use of hand signs. With periods of time a hand, usually open, marks completion; the back of a hand or closed fist over *kin*, sun or day, is west, clearly with the meaning 'day completed' (Fig. 4 *r*). Terms for west or sunset vary so much from Maya group to Maya group that a phonetic rendering is unlikely.

The term for hand in Yucatec and other lowland languages is *kab*, which is also a verb meaning to make something with one's hands. The back of a fist with a T-shaped *Ik* sign, and a postfix indicating adoration – *tzil?*, is the glyph of the Chacs, the all-important rain gods. *Ik* signifies wind, breath and, by extension, life. In agricultural almanacs are pictured two-leafed maize plants growing from it, obviously illustrating that aspect of life which we call germination. A glyph carrying the idea of makers of germination or of life in general is very appropriate for the Chacs who cause the crops to grow. Among the many titles of the Chacs occurs *Ah Tzenulob* (recorded as *Ah Dz'enulob*, surely an error). The term means 'The Nourishers' or 'The Sustainers' and conveys a similar idea, but the pictogram is ideographic, not phonetic (Fig. 4 *s*, *t*).

Itzam Na, god of creation, the sky and the earth, personification of the soil and vegetation, was more important even than the Chacs. A common glyph of that four-fold deity is his head with the symbol for vegetal growth (*bil*) emerging from a sort of inset or cavity in his forehead. In the latter an oval occurs against the inner edge. The whole, I think, represents the sprouting of a maize seed set in the god's forehead (Fig. 4 *w*). This conforms well with the idea that the god, in one of his aspects, personifies the soil. Again, a pictogram is ideographic; it conveys the function of the god, not his name.

6. Pictograms with secondary phonetic values are not uncommon, and one may conjecture that with further research their number will grow. The *bil*, vegetation, affix has been mentioned. An inspection of sculpture makes clear that this is a somewhat formalized representation of two leaves of a maize plant (it is often set in the headdress of the maize god with an ear of maize rising from it). It appears to correspond to *bil*; *bilmal* – *mal*, become, converts nouns into verbs – is to grow or sprout applied to maize or other plants. Attached to the *kan*, maize, glyph (Fig. 4 *f*), it indicates growing or tender near-ripe maize (*nal* in Yucatec), whereas the plain *kan* sign represents *ixim*, fully ripe maize, particularly after removal from the cob. Often *bil* is attached to the *pop*, reed mat, glyph, presumably to indicate its vegetal origin. In such cases *bil* is ideographic (Fig. 8).

However, *bil* is attached to many glyphs where the value vegetation will not fit. In such cases it is to be read phonetically as the participial suffix *bil*. A form of inverted hand apparently stands for *dẓ'a*, give; with *bil* affix postfixed it becomes *dẓ'abil*, given (Fig. 4 *u*). Another hand compound seems to correspond to *tanlah*, serve, as to serve God; with *bil* it becomes *tanlahbil*, served (Fig. 5 *s*).

The conventionalized picture of the moon indicates the moon or its age, that is with, say, 12 before it, it records that the current moon is 12 days old. With a very small change, not observed in the hieroglyphic books, the moon sign stands for 20. Terms for 20 vary according to the objects enumerated, but the commonest in both lowland and highland Maya tongues is *kal*.

A moon sign is very frequently postfixed to certain glyphs and the compounds thus formed without serious doubt serve as verbs. It is a very ancient form for it appears on the earliest stelae. In Manche Chol *kal* means to do or make; in Putun, with the same meaning, but as a noun, it converts nouns and adjectives into verbs; in Chorti which replaces lowland *l* with *r kare* is to do; the word is near extinction in Yucatec, but survives, for instance, in *kalal*, making. Here, then, is a very old moon postfix possibly corresponding to an archaic term *kal* which converts nouns and adjectives into verbs, but, as in other very old forms, the interpretation is not certain (Pl. 5 first glyph of each *t'ol*; Figs. 2, A8, D6, 3 *h*, 5 *s*).

7. Metaphorgrams are glyphs which correspond to figures of speech or recognized symbols. The *cuch*, burden, glyph with the meaning fate or destiny, and the wood and stone affixes meaning strife are examples already discussed. The shield and the jaguar (once the day sign *Ix* used for jaguar) are symbols of war, and are used glyphically as such (Figs. 3 *m*, 4 *k*). Jaguar skin, because of its markings, was a metaphor for night sky and is used in that sense in glyphic texts (Fig. 6 *e*).

The bat head as a symbol of sacrifice (blood-spilling) has been noted; a much more interesting case is the head of a bat placed upside down before a time period to mark its end. In Maya thought time was an unending march into the future; the periods of time were thought of as bearing on their backs the number attached to the current period. For example, during Katun 18, the katun (20 vague-year period) was the traveller, the number 18 was his burden. At the end of the katun, when the traveller came to rest, he set down his burden of 18; next morning, when he started off again, he carried instead number 19 because Katun 19 had begun.

As a bat at rest hangs head down, it is not far-fetched to suppose that this was a striking way of illustrating that the period had come to rest. In fact, the Palencano Chol Maya who still inhabit the area around the great Classic-period site of Palenque, where the glyph of the upside-down bat probably originated, speak figuratively of a tired man as 'very bat face'. Perhaps this arose from the head of an exhausted man drooping so much that he was jestingly called bat head. In any case this is surely a most imaginative metaphorgram of the period coming to rest after its long march (Fig. 4 *d*).

Hatz in Yucatec is to part; *haatzal caan*, parting of the sky, and *hatz cab*, earth parting or splitting, are metaphorical expressions for dawn and morning respectively. On the monuments of the Classic period a compound sign which can be shown to function in counting days comprises a small sun glyph wedged in the angle between two diverging signs. The lower which is horizontal is the earth (*cab*) glyph; the upper, tilted at an angle of 45°, is the sky (*caan*) glyph. Clearly the whole pictures earth and sky parting to let the sun rise (Fig. 4 *x, y*). That the glyph corresponds to the metaphor is put beyond question by one example in which both upper and lower arms of the angle are *cab*, earth, glyphs. The compound depicts the earth dividing at sunrise, *hatzcab*, to allow the sun to emerge.

Jade was the most valued possession of all peoples of Middle America, and, together with quetzal feathers which were equally coveted, served as a figure of speech to denote anything very precious. Water was regarded also as very precious and as bodies of water were of the same colour (the Maya used a single term for green and blue), the jade symbol served as the glyph for water (Fig. 7, Muluc). Blood, too, was a precious substance since it fed the gods. It is surely for that reason that sometimes in scenes of human sacrifice feathers rise from the cavity in the breast made when the heart was excised; they represent the spurting blood.

8. Attributive glyphs, that is glyphs which identify a deity by one or more of his or her attributes, occur. A special affix deriving from the headdress which distinguishes the gods called Bacabs has been mentioned. A compound consisting of the number four (four dots), this attributive affix and the *cauac* sign, here to be taken in its sense of *ku*, god, reads 'the Four gods, the Bacabs', or 'the Four Bacab gods'. The Bacabs were always known as *the* Four gods. This same attributive affix may be placed above a personal attribute of a Bacab, notably a conch shell or turtle shell because one Bacab bears on his back a conch shell or emerges from it whereas another wears a turtle shell as though it were a cuirass. Again, prefixed to the *kin* sign, it reads 'Festival of the Bacabs' (Fig. 4 *a, a'–c'*).

The wife of the creator, known as Ix Chebel Yax or as 'Lady Unique, Owner of Cloth, Owner of the (red) Paint Brush', in reference to her patronage of weaving, brocading, and painting sundry objects red, is portrayed in the hieroglyphic books, usually with face and body painted red. Her glyph is the *men*, worker or craftsman, glyph with the red affix and a hank of cotton added. Alternatively, an aged head with the red affix identifies her. Both red and hank of cotton serve here as attributive glyphs to distinguish this aged goddess of creation (Figs. 4 *d', e'*, 5 *a*).

Similarly, a somewhat conventionalized, but recognizable trader's pack serves as a glyph to identify merchant gods; it is purely attributive, and has no phonetic value (Fig. 5 *g*).

9. 'Determinative' is applied to a glyphic element which indicates in case of doubt in what sense the main sign to which it is attached should be read. Two determinatives have already been mentioned (p. 49): addition of the *te*, wood, affix or the mat element to the *cuch* glyph determines whether the main sign is to be read as burden hence destiny or as seat of authority (Fig. 3 *a'–b'*).

The day sign *Caban* with a certain suffix (No. 251) replacing the cartouche stands for *cab*, a Yucatec term for honey and also earth (but now surviving only in compounds). This *cab* (with suffix 251) may itself serve as a determinative. *Balche*, in Yucatec, signifies both an inhabitant of the forest, hence game, and a tree (*Lonchocarpus longostylus*), the bark of which is added to honey to hasten fermentation. The resulting mead, the principal alcoholic drink of the Maya, was also termed *balche*. In some passages dealing with food offerings the *cab* glyph is added to that for *balche* to indicate that mead is the offering; elsewhere – for instance, below pictures of ensnared deer – the *bak*, flesh, sign is joined to the *balche* sign to make clear that the latter is being used in the sense of game (Fig. 5 *h, i*).

10. Religious ideas in glyph formation. The most obvious example of religion or myth in Maya writing is the use on occasions of portraits of different gods to represent the numbers 1 to 13 (Fig. 7) in place of the usual system of circles to represent numbers 1 to 4 and a straight line to indicate 5 (e.g., 19 was written as 4 circles and 3 straight lines). This use of the heads of gods to represent numbers arises from a very old belief that numbers were divine beings, and that divine rank extended also to each of the 20 days; each day was not just under the influence of a particular god, it was that god. As examples of deity-number relations, deities of moon, sun, jaguar, maize, death, and earth were lords of numbers 1, 4, 7, 8, 10 and 11 respectively. Occasionally, the process is reversed: 4 circles or dots written to represent the sun in non-numerical contexts (Pl. 6, *T'ol* 8, Glyph 3) or three circles and a bar replace the head of the maize god (Fig. 5 *l*). Portraits of gods may substitute for the symbolic day signs they personify (Fig. 7, Chicchan, Cimi) or the characteristic feature of the day sign may be infixed on the cheek (Fig. 7, *Ik*). Rarely, a god's head may replace an associated affix: the god of nine who normally

wears the *yax* affix on his forehead once substitutes for the *yax* (new) affix in the *yax hatzcab*, new dawn, compound (Fig. 4 *y*, *z*).

The Maya made use of rebus writing to overcome the difficulty of expressing abstract ideas. The use of the head of a mythical shark-like fish called *xoc* to represent the homonym *xoc*, count or to count, supplies an interesting example. In the inscriptions of the Classic period intervals, expressed in years, months and days, are very frequently counted forward or backward from one date to another. With these calculations appear the head of this shark deity distinguished by prominent barbules and dorsal fin set at back of head. Certain affixes establish whether the count is forward (Fig. 2, C2 left, E7) or backward (Fig. 6 *g–i*).

Frequently the water (originally jade) sign, with precisely the same affixes, replaces the *xoc* head in these passages (Figs. 2, C5, F1; 6 *g*). Presumably, this was simplification or a time-saving device applied to a much repeated compound: the complex *xoc* head was difficult to carve; the water-jade sign is severely simple. *Xoc* was the augury of the day *Muluc*, water, and water, in turn, as the habitat of fish, is a natural allegory for a fish deity. Here jade represents water which stands for *xoc*, shark, which, in turn, serves for its homonym *xoc*, to count, an illustration of the impediments to decipherment.

11. The *pars pro toto* presentation had wide acceptance among Maya scribes. In nearly all cases heads, almost always in profile, represent gods and animals. Quite rarely – usually when the grandeur of the passage of time was the occasion – full-length portraits occur, although 'full-length' hardly fits the manner in which limbs are bent, twisted and intertwined to conform to available space (frontispiece). The part-for-whole process can be carried further: a jaguar ear with the animal's characteristic markings stands for the whole animal (Fig. 5 *m–o*); what is almost surely the hoof of a deer represents the

whole animal because *mai*, hoof, is a liturgical name for deer. More-over, it is probable that, as in Nahuatl imagery, deer hoof stands for speed (Fig. 5 *p*). Similarly, a jaguar paw and foreleg affix (Fig. 5 *k*) almost certainly stands for jaguar – by extension, war – because *chacmol*, large paw, is the common Yucatec term for jaguar.

12. Affixes may represent speech particles attached to nominal or verbal roots. Examples are *al* (23) postfixed to *caan*, sky, or *yax*, green, to produce *caanal*, on high (Fig. 3 *j*), or *yaxal*, greenish; the relationship *il* (24) added to *tun* to read *tunil*, connected with a *tun* (360-day year) (Fig. 4 *o*); the past participial *bil* (130) joined to a verbal root as in *u kochbil* (1.19:130) to record her perched on or *tanlahbil* (74:669:130) served or worshipped (Fig. 5 *q, s*). These last examples, perhaps not accepted by all students, are given to illustrate roots modified by both prefix and postfix. There was probably a postfix, still unidentified, to represent the prophetic future (*om* in Yucatec), but one may doubt the existence of affixes to distinguish singular from plural, personal pronouns other than the third person, and present from past tense.

13. In speech the Maya liked to play on like-sounding words and there is some evidence that they did the same in hieroglyphic texts. In sections covering the medicinal activities of the moon goddess, texts and supplementary pictures referring to *koch*, disease, and its homonym to bear on one's shoulders, appear beside others treating of *cuch*, burden carried on one's back and, by extension, fate or destiny. Here there is a play on sounds, *koch* and *cuch*, shoulder burden harmonizing with back burden, as well as use of homonyms. In the first three sections of the almanac on *Dresden*, pp. 13 *b*–14 *b*, the first glyph reads *u tanlah*, his taking care of; the second is the maize glyph qualified as green or new by the addition of the *bil* (130) affix. In the last three sections the *bil* affix is transferred to the *tanlah*

glyph where it serves as the participial postfix *bil*, to form *tanlahbil*, taken care of. In other words there is a switch from active to passive and the *bil* affix achieves this by changing from an indicator of fresh vegetal growth to an indicator of the passive participle, both expressed by *bil*. It is a neat play on sounds with an almost contrapuntal effect (Fig. 5 *r–s*). The compound of a doubled *ca* (25) affix with *bil* postfixed (Fig. 3 *i*) was identified as the cacao sign by Cyrus Thomas seventy years ago. Here *bil* is a determinative, indicating that *caca* is here to be read as cacao, not as *caca*, by twos or by pairs.

14. Portrait and symbolic forms. Many Maya terms including some represented by affixes may be expressed either as profile heads or as symbols, the latter usually somewhat conventionalized representations of an attribute or characteristic of the subject of the corresponding portrait. This is true of most day signs, numbers and time periods. As all three classes were regarded as divine beings, the use of portraits is understandable. The substitution of symbolic forms helps analysis of the religious soil in which the glyphs were rooted, but as the discussion below makes plain, gaps are many and wide in our knowledge of Maya beliefs and myths of two millennia ago. Portrait glyphs are far commoner in early texts; as writing expanded they were increasingly replaced by symbolic forms, presumably because the latter were more quickly carved or written; and because one attribute of a god could be used in one sense or context and another in another, expansion did not reduce intelligibility.

As numbers and days were divine beings, portraits of the corresponding gods served to represent the numbers one to thirteen (above thirteen the Maya employed a 'teens' system as we do) and, in addition a sequence of thirteen days, starting, not with the first day, *Imix*, but for an unknown reason with *Caban*, the seventeenth day. The symbolic forms of the days derive from some attribute or association

Deity of	Portrait characteristic	No.	Day name	Meaning	Characteristic of 1 symbol, 2 portrait
Moon	Hair lock on cheek[1]	1	*Caban*	Earth	1 hair lock like our ?, 2 moon goddess
Sacrifice	Hand over head	2	*Etz'nab*	Biting, cutting implement	1 flint blade, 2 only one weathered example
Rain	T wind, life sign on cheek or in earplug	3	*Cauac*	Rain storm	1 rain sign often with T, head with above in eye
Sun	Squint, often sun glyph also	4	*Ahau*	Lord	1 Face of blowgunner,[2] 2 Young sun god
Old Bacab, sky sustainer	Tun (year) sign headdress	5	*Imix*	*Imix*, earth god	1 Water lily,[3] 2 earth aspect of Itzam Na
A rain god	Axe in eye[4]	6	*Ik*	Wind, breath, life	1 T life sign, 2 same on cheek or earplug
Jaguar of night sky, underworld	Loop under eyes twisted over nose[5]	7	*Akbal*	Darkness	1 loop under eyes, black spots, 2 none
Maize	Maize grains; curl of *bil* on forehead[6]	8	*Kan*	Maize	1 Sign often in maize god's headdress, 2 one only, no characteristic
Rain *Chicchan*	*Yax* on forehead; jaguar spots and whiskers[7]	9	*Chicchan*	Snake	1 *Yax* sign, 2 head with snake markings
Death	Skull. May have % sign	10	*Cimi*	Death	1 % sign (very rare), 2 skull
Earth (God R)	earth curl and number 11	11	*Manik*	?	1 grasping hand, 2 none
Venus?	Sky sign headdress[8]	12	*Lamat*	?	1 Venus sign, 2 Venus god
Itzam Na earth aspect	Long-nosed with earth signs	13	*Muluc*	?	1 water or jade, 2 only one has water symbol

[1] Lock of hair is female symbol; as moon goddess is also earth deity, it stands also for earth.
[2] Round mouth suggests the blowgun in using which the young sun god excelled.
[3] The earth rested on a crocodile in a great lagoon which the water lily represents.
[4] an axe was the symbol of the rain gods called Chacs.
[5] Often the number 7 is on the god's cheek.
[6] The curl under *pars pro toto* rule stands for *bil*, vegetation.
[7] Jaguar is a rain deity in Olmec culture. In one case the god of nine replaces the *yax* affix in a compound, evidence of the close connection (Fig. 4 *y*, *z*).
[8] The principal Venus god was called Lahun Chan, 10 Sky.

of the corresponding god. This sequence is presented (left) in tabular form because it splendidly illustrates the way in which religion dominated the Maya calendar (Fig. 7); only Yucatec day names are given – other Maya groups had variant day names – because they are customarily used in discussing the calendar, and partly to simplify the presentation, although in some cases archaic day names, retained in other lists, are lost in the Yucatec sequence.

Meanings of some day names are – to use a trite expression – lost in antiquity and the same is true of some divine associations. In some cases one can guess at missing links, as, for instance, in the case of god of number two with hand above head and *Etz'nab*. That day name apparently means an implement for biting or tearing; the symbol is a flint knife. Aztec representations of flint knives often have an inset mouth with prominent teeth seemingly to convey that idea. Among the Maya the sacrificial knife used to cut out human hearts was called the hand of god, which may be the explanation of the hand above the god's head. Again, in day names from other Maya groups (here omitted to simplify presentation) *Manik*'s equivalent is termed deer, and the corresponding Aztec day is both called deer and is pictured as one. Why the Maya used a grasping hand to denote the day is unknown.

The head of a frog or toad is the portrait form of the uinal (20-day month) (Fig. 2, A3). Here again, speculation gives an insight into possible lines of decipherment. In some lunar texts an upended head, apparently of a frog or toad (Fig. 1 *b*, B6), may substitute for the regular moon sign, which, as we have seen, in turn, has the value twenty. *Po* is the term for moon among the Kekchi and Pokom highland Maya and is part of the corresponding terms in neighbouring non-Maya languages (e.g., Zoque), but it is also an element in names of toads or frogs in certain Maya languages including Palencano Chol.

It is possible, therefore, that here we have a case of rebus writing developed before writing spread from the highland Maya to the lowlands. Then to complicate matters, moon-twenty-*kal* (p. 55) forms an independent grouping of homonyms with lunar associations.

As examples of portrait forms of symbolic affixes one may note the following.

A naturalistic fish occasionally replaces the comb (25) affix in the common *Imix*-comb-*Imix* compound (Fig. 5 *t–u*). The head of a fish with prominent barbules and dorsal fin serves as the portrait of the *xoc* shark, used as rebus for *xoc*, to count. Its normal form is a very flattened affix which represents the same mythical fish. An attribute of the death god is an arrangement of the hair set with eyes, and this is the origin of Affix 12, with the probable meaning *hidz'*, expiration. Often a little death head takes its place (Fig. 5 *w*, *x*).

15. Compression and expansion of compound glyphs. Glyphic elements could be suppressed to save space either in a long passage or to reduce crowding within a single glyph block, but some detail of the suppressed glyph had to be retained so as not to obscure the meaning of the whole compound.

Normally the sign corresponding to *haab*, year, was the *cauac*, rain storm, sign plus Affix 116 which usually is postfixed to the *kin*, sun, glyph (Fig. 6 *a*). It resembles a number of cords and probably represents the sun's rays, a Yucatec term for which was *tab*, cord. *Cauac* with Affix 116 signifies rain and sun, in other words the two seasons into which the tropical year is divided. The *kin* is suppressed the *tab* cords are sufficient to convey the information. This, of course, is an ideogram.

The very common Prefix 168 comprising two elements (Fig. 6 *d–f*) corresponds, I believe, to *ah*, the masculine prefix but this also means lord and is used to denote one who follows a trade, e.g. *col*, milpa, corn field; *ah col*, one who makes milpa, a farmer. Similarly *zacal* is to weave; *ah zacal* is a woman who weaves. The prefix is very ancient and is probably of highland Maya origin for one of its elements is the day sign called *Ben* in Yucatec, but which corresponds to *Ah* in highland Maya lists of day names.

Ah prefix and *nal* suffix in Yucatec indicate owner. *Ah col nal* is the owner of a milpa. Many glyphs have Prefix 168 and postfix *bil* (130). As we have seen, the maize sign with the *bil* sign indicates green maize or unripe ears of maize, our corn on the cob, a favourite Maya dish; without the affix the glyph means ripe or dry maize in general (*ixim*). When, therefore, both the *ah* and this *bil* prefix which converts maize from *ixim* to *nal* are present, it is a fair assumption that they stand for *ah . . . nal*, and that the maize sign itself is suppressed. The name glyph of the sun god is written as the sun sign with this same 168 and 130 combination (Fig. 6 *d*). If the above interpretation is accepted, the whole reads *ah kin nal*, Owner or Lord of the sun, a fair enough way of writing the sun god's name, although his regular title in Yucatec was *Kinich Ahau*, Sun-face lord. Note that in the name glyph the sun-rays postfix is suppressed partly to save crowding, but in fact he was lord of the sun, not of the sun and its rays unless one wants to be pedantic. Lord of the divine bat with additional aquatic symbols (Fig. 6 *f*) was the emblem glyph of Copan.

Glyph 609 represents the spotted skin of a jaguar, which in turn stands for throne because a jaguar skin was placed on a ruler's seat and also for the night sky which poetically was regarded as a jaguar skin, the spots being the stars. With the same affixes 168 and 130, the whole is a title: Lord (owner) of the Jaguar Skin or Lord of the Night Sky (Fig. 6 *e*). This is not a fanciful identification; there is good supporting evidence in literature, glyphic texts, sculpture and Aztec sources. This illustrates the decipherer's need for a full knowledge of all aspects of Middle American culture for a connection between jaguar skin and ruler or night sky is far from obvious.

Another space-saving device was to suppress an affix or one of a pair of main signs of a compound and infix the characteristic features of the suppressed element in the surviving main sign. For example, the characteristic of the month *Ch'en* is its black prefix. This could be infixed within the main (*cauac*) sign, but on becoming an infix, its characteristic cross-hatching is no longer confined within an affix outline (Fig. 3 *a–c*). As remarked (p. 51), the heart and bat signs are often combined to represent human sacrifice, but the heart could be suppressed, and its chief characteristics, the aorta and the death eyelash, infixed in the bat head (Fig. 3 *r–t*). Similarly, the seating affix of the seating of the *haab* glyph could be infixed in the *haab*, the latter identified by the cords postfix and context (Fig. 6 *b*, *c*). The postfix of the *cab*, earth, part of the milpa compound, could similarly be infixed (Fig. 4 *e*).

Compounds were at times expanded to fill two glyph blocks. When that occurred, were there a prefix for the whole compound, this appeared with each half of the sign after splitting. Affix 267, signifying something like malevolent or evil, over the *kin* (sun) and *tun* signs means evil or harmful excessive sun (*tun*, year or stone, is used here for its homonym *tun*, excessive). When the compound is expanded, Affix 267 is placed over each sign (Fig. 5 *d–f*). The same is true of the milpa (corn field) compound if that is expanded to occupy two blocks.

16. Affixes and main signs may change places particularly when the former are personified. In one interesting example of the count-backward compound following a distance number at Quirigua (Thompson, 1950, Fig. 4, No. 29) the count element becomes the fish prefix (Affix 204), the locative prefix *ti*, meaning to, at or from, is personified

as a vulture on becoming the main sign (note Fig. 5 *v* and caption). One sees that the sculptor or his sacerdotal employer took full advantage of the artistic licence permitted him, and introduced the little play on associations *ti-ta* locative with excrement homonym and the vulture's nickname of excrement head (*ta hol*). A parallel in our culture would be the sly, joking scenes on misericords. Had we not the clues of context and the *ti-ta*-excrement play on words, it would, indeed, have been difficult to read this compound. One feels that a computer would have blown a fuse in exasperating failure to solve that problem.

The so-called Glyph F which forms a clause with Glyph G, naming the current Lord of the Night, is composed of three affixes, the lower two of which, a knot and the *al* suffix, are very probably to be read as *tabal*, companion (p. 71; Fig. 1*a*, A6), a term applied to those lords of the nights in the Valley of Mexico. However, the *al* suffix may be personified as a youthful deity, and when that happens, it is promoted to be a main sign with the other elements affixed to it.

Another example of an affix becoming a main sign on personification is a *ca*, comb, postfix which achieves main sign status on being personified as a fish, *cai* in Yucatec (Fig. 3 *f, g*).

Additional examples of the above 'rules' appear in the illustrations.

Wider considerations

Clearly, many allusions to religious beliefs, myth and folklore are embodied in Maya writing just as they are in medieval Christian iconography. Some of the imagery, comparable, so to speak, to St Barbara's tower or St Thomas' doubt or Raleigh's cloak, comes within our knowledge; other items, within the ken of the faithful, are unrecognized by us and are hardly likely to shed their allegorical cloaks when bedded with the unadventurous computer.

Those who fashioned Maya writing certainly knew that there is more than one way to skin a cat. Context and practice would inform a priest which way a glyph should be read, whether, for example, a *tun* sign should be read as year, stone, or excessive, or a moon sign as moon, twenty or *kal*, action. A priest would have no difficulty in recognizing religious imagery in glyphs and he could draw on a wider background to detect a metaphor or identify the characteristic of some animal head.

I have thought that a Maya writing glyphs might be compared to a man speaking in a foreign tongue of which he does not have full mastery; both persons resort to circumlocution to express their thoughts. However, hieroglyphic texts were above all the bones on which a priest moulded the flesh of oratory. Bishop Landa tells how a priest expounded from his hieroglyphic book the auguries for the incoming year. Such texts survive. In *Codex Dresden* the prophecies for each year require only some thirty glyph blocks; in *Codex Madrid* they fill about fifty glyph blocks. Obviously, then, the text was, so to speak, a prompt book or list of headings, on which the high priest, being also a political leader, no doubt discoursed at unconscionable length, as is the way of parsons and politicians the world over.

In compensating for their limited range of glyphs, the Maya ingeniously utilized ideograms, pictograms, synonyms, but, above all rebus writing to express themselves.

Many glyphs are still undeciphered, but because of the varying ways in which so many could be used, I doubt that unchallenged decipherment of all texts will ever be achieved, particularly where very early glyphs, such as day signs, are concerned, for they have attracted so many related ideas. For instance, *Imix*, first of the twenty days, has associations with earth, water, water lilies, crocodiles, plenty, vegetation and beginning; the problem is what particular aspect is relevant in a given situation.

Again, the absence of so many old terms with religious connotations from Maya-Spanish vocabularies is a serious handicap. The Maya knew better than to reveal such terms to the word-collecting friars; knowledge of old pagan practices could get an informant into trouble. Apart from that serious drawback, good linguistic material exists for Yucatec Maya, but for the whole southern lowlands there is only one early vocabulary, and that of limited value.

Exercises in decipherment

In this final section, examples of better understood passages will be examined. The first text is an Initial Series and lunar series, so called because, with few exceptions, it stands at the start of inscriptions carved on monuments of the Classic period. It is a record of the time elapsed from a starting point (equivalent to 10 August, 3113 B.C.) projected back far into the past, and is in the vigesimal system, used in all Maya counting, whether of years, loads of corn, linear measurements or cacao beans which served as currency. The unit was the *tun*, a 'year' of 360 days (they also used a 365-day year of 18 'months', called *uinals*, of twenty days each plus a very unlucky five-day period at the end). Twenty tuns formed a katun (a contraction of *kaltun*, 20 tuns) and 20 *katuns* were a *baktun* (*bak* signifies 400). For periods less than a *tun* 'fractions' were used: 18 *uinals* of 20 days each and days. All periods were numbered 1 to 19 with the last day called completion. In our notation this is written as a zero, but in fact the sign does not mean zero or nothing, but completion. Completion of one period could also be expressed as the seating of the next. The count of an Initial Series is in descending order.

At the head of an Initial Series is what we call the introductory glyph, usually occupying the space of two or even four glyph blocks. The Maya name for this may have been *xoctun*, count of the *tuns*. It comprises a tun sign with flanking *xoc*, fish, elements, and in the upper centre a variable element, the portrait or symbol of the god or goddess who ruled over the 20-day month in which the recorded date fell. Texts are read in the usual way in pairs left to right in descending order.

Normally clauses giving information on the regnant lord of the night (there were nine who ruled in fixed sequence which repeated unendingly) and lunar matters intervene between the glyph of the day reached and the corresponding month position.

The first example (Fig. 1 *a*) is inscribed on a jamb of the doorway of Temple 18, Palenque. Part of the jamb was found by Maudslay in 1891; the greater part by Alberto Ruz in 1954. It records with numerical bars and dots and symbolic forms of the periods an Initial Series which we transcribe as 9.12.6.5.8 3 *Lamat* 6 *Zac* corresponding to 14 September A.D. 678 The temple commemorated a date perhaps 43 years later. The text reads:

A1–B2: Initial Series introductory glyph (*xoctun?*, count of the *tuns*). The variable element in the centre is the head of the patron of the month *Zac*, a long-nosed deity. The sign occupies the space of four glyph blocks.

A3: 9 (1 bar and 4 dots) *baktuns*. Note how the right *cauac* sign partly covers the left one. It signifies 9 × 400 *tuns*.

B3: 12 (two bars and two dots separated by an ornamental bow) *katuns*. This is a *tun* glyph surmounted by a *cauac* flanked by 'combs'. It signifies 12 × 20 *tuns*.

A4: 6 (bar and 1 dot flanked by ornamental bows) *tuns* (360-day years).

B4: 5 (1 bar) *te uinals* (20-day months). *Te* is a numerical classifier used with periods of time – *hote uinalob* in Maya. Usually it was omitted in writing.

A5: 8 (1 bar and 3 dots) *kins* (days), the glyph of the sun with the cord (sun's rays) suffix. The count, then, is 3,600+240+6, a total of 3,846 *tuns* plus 108 days from the starting point.

B5: 3 *Lamat*, day of Venus, the day reached by the calculation. The glyph is the Venus sign.

Last glyph, the month position 8 *Zac*. In the original this sign is separated from the day sign not only by the lunar series but also by another series of glyphs not discussed here. It has been moved up to follow the last glyph of the lunar series. *Zac* consists of the *zac* (white) prefix to left, a knot above and a *cauac* sign as main element.

A6, left: head of the old sun god as lord of the current night; right: this compound forms a clause with the glyph of the lord of the night (indeed, the latter is often infixed in it). In Central Mexico the lords of the nights were called 'the accompanied ones'. The main elements comprise a knot and the *al* suffix. In a full figure compound the lord of the night carries the night, depicted as a rolled-up jaguar skin (Frontispiece B4; see p. 55 for jaguar skin as night symbol) by means of a tump line with a conspicuous knot at the front. In Yucatec, Chorti and Palencano Chol both tump and cord are called *tab*, giving a reading of *tabal*, which in Yucatec means companion in a group. In all likelihood the knot and *al* contain the same idea of companionhood of the lords of the nights as on the Mexican plateau.

B6: here begins a clause giving lunar data. The number 19 is present as well as the upturned toad head which can substitute for the moon sign (p. 63). The whole records that at the date of the Initial Series the current moon was 19 days old.

A7: this compound, known as Glyph C of the lunar series, here with a numerical bar, states that the fifth lunation of the series has been completed or is current. The former is preferable because the outstretched hand normally indicates completion. At the right is the right half of the moon sign, the left half is suppressed presumably to save space. Above the hand is a pack (Glyph 680). As an attribute of the merchant gods, it indicates that they or their leader were patrons of the recorded lunation.

B7: this is called Glyph X of the series because it is a variable. There are some eight distinctive forms, that shown depending on the number of lunations and the patron of the previous Glyph C. The combination of fifth lunation and merchant's pack calls for the form here shown. Conceivably the forms of Glyph X represent constellations.

A8: Glyph B of the series, an animal with pointed snout, perhaps a coati, is within an elbow with the crossed bands of conjunction infixed. It forms a clause with Glyph X (in one text the supposed coati carries Glyph X on his back). As a guess, X and B record that the moon is in conjunction with a constellation, the animal head representing the action.

B8: Glyph A, the moon sign here with value 20 with two numerical bars attached informs us that the current or last completed lunation was of 30 days. A lunation is 29·53 days; the Maya roughly alternated moons of 30 and 29 days.

In the second Initial and lunar series (Fig. 1 *b*) both numbers and periods are expressed with portraits. It is from a drawing published by Maudslay of part of Stela F, Quirigua, and reads 9.16.10.0.0 1 *A hau* 3 *Zip*, corresponding to 15 March 761 A.D., 3930 tuns from the starting point.

A1–B2: Initial Series introductory glyph. The fret-nosed creature without lower jaw is an earth aspect of the great god Itzam Na, Iguana House, patron of the month *Zip*.

A3: 9 *baktuns*. The head for 9 on the left has the characteristic jaguar spots of that god. The *baktun* has a hand over the lower jaw, its distinguishing feature. the artist had considerable latitude in carving these period glyphs since they are identifiable by their positions in the sequence.

B3: 16 *katuns*. The head combines the axe in the eye of 6 with the jawbone and % sign of the death god, patron of number 10. The *katun* head is distinguished by the pendulous nose and the hollow in the top of the head.

A4: 10 *tuns*. The head for ten has the same attributes of the death god, jawbone and % sign. The *tun* sign also has as its characteristic the fleshless lower jaw.

B4: 0 *uinals*. The head for completion on the left has a hand, sign for completion, over lower jaw. The toad, recognizable by the curl at the back of the mouth and the three circlets, representing the creature's poison glands, portrays the 20-day month (see p. 63).

A5: 0 *kins* (days). The same head for completion as in B4. The head has the filed central incisors of the sun (*kin*) god and the rather weathered headdress probably once displayed the *kin* sign.

B5: 1 *Ahau*, the day reached. The head for one is that of the moon goddess, but her attribute, the lock of hair, is partly masked by another element. *Ahau* is the portrait of the young sun god.

A6, left half: again the sun god as lord of the night. The cross hachure of the *kin* in the headdress indicates blackness. At night the sun traversed the underworld to reappear in the east at sunrise; right half: the personified form of the companion sign (Glyph F).

B6, left: a unique beaked head, what might be a pendent wattle suggests a turkey. Right: the upended toad head represents the moon. Absence of a number indicates no lunar age, that is conjunction.

A7: Glyph C recording 6 lunations with a youthful patron.

B7: Glyph X variant appropriate for six lunations and a youthful patron. On the left the sky sign stands above the earth; to right a long-nosed god with *cauac* headdress.

A8: Glyph A, the moon representing 20 and the death god (note the prominent jawbone) personifying 10. It is a 30-day lunation.

B8: 3 *Zip*. The head for 3 (T-sign in ear and typical tam-o-shanter) and the month *Zip*. In the Manche Chol calendar this month is called *Chac Kat*, red conjunction. This term corresponds to the glyph for the superfix is the sign for *chac* red, and cross bands are *kat*, conjunction.

Very often several dates additional to the Initial Series were recorded on a monument. These are usually linked together by what are termed distance numbers so that their positions in terms of the starting point were established without repeating their positions by means of the long Initial Series. In distance numbers the periods are almost invariably recorded with symbolic forms and almost invariably arranged in ascending order in contrast to the descending order of Initial Series.

The first example (Fig. 2) is found on Stela 3, Piedras Negras. There are four distance numbers (henceforward written D.N.) leading from an Initial Series to the end of a *katun*, the dedicatory date of the stela. The arrangement in our notations:

A1–B7:	9.12. 2. 0.16	5 *Cib*, lunar series, 14 *Yaxkin*
C1–C2a:	12.10. 0	D.N., forward count to
C2b–D2a:	[9.12.14.10.16]	1 *Cib* 14 *Kankin*
D4–C5:	1. 1.11.10	D.N., forward count to
D5–C6:	[9.13.16. 4. 6]	4 *Cimi* 14 *Uo*
E1–F1:	3. 8.15	D.N., forward count to
E2–F2:	[9.13.19.13. 1]	11 *Imix* 14 *Yax*
F4–E5:		Completion expiration 5 *haab*, 1 *katun*
F6–E7:	4.19	D.N., forward count to
F7–F10:	[9.14. 0. 0. 0]	6 *Ahau* 13 *Muan*, completion 14th *katun*

Material in brackets is not in the original, but is easily calculated. The Initial Series date corresponds to A.D. 5 July 674; the last date to 3 December A.D. 711 The head of the introductory glyph is the sun god's, patron of the month *Yaxkin* (note the *kin* sign over the ear). The Initial Series combines bar and dot numerals with portraits of the periods. B4 is the seventh lord of the nights as here required. The lunar series records a moon age of 27 days (B5), 2 lunations (A6), a form of Glyph X corresponding to 2 lunations and the death god patron (B6), and a 29-day moon (A7).

As usual in D.N.s the *kin* sign is suppressed and its number attached

to the *uinal*. Generally a glyph standing for *hel*, change, introduces
each D.N. (Pl. 2 *b*), but it is absent on this stela. A special suffix (two
circles between loops) differentiates periods in D.N.s (D1, D4, C5,
E1). C2*a* reads, top to bottom, forward (or some similar expression)
count, to. Count, *xoc*, is here carved as a stylized head of the *xoc* fish
(p. 59); the suffix is the locative *ti*, to, at or from. In the corresponding
compound with the next D.N. (C5*b*) the water symbol replaces the
xoc head and the *ti* sign is in alternative postfixal position to the right.
In the fourth D.N. the *xoc* head again appears, but the forward affix
is to the left (E7).

Completion expiration of 5th *haab*, 1 *katun* (F4–E5) calls attention
to the accompanying date being the 25th *tun* anniversary of another
(9.12.14.13.1 7 *Imix* 19 *Pax*) on the side of this stela, apparently
the accession date of a ruler marked by F5*a*. The bracket over the 5,
as well as that to the left of 14 *katuns* (F10) has the sound value *u*.
In Maya speech it converts cardinals to ordinals. The hand expresses
completion (F4*a*, F9). Of the 48 glyph blocks, $33\frac{1}{2}$ are calendrical;
the rest, not discussed, inform on historical (and perhaps other)
matters.

The narrow front of Lintel 25, Yaxchilan, now in the British
Museum, shows glyph carving at its finest (Pl. 4). Calendrical
material comprises a D.N. counted from a date on the underside.
Note the *hel*, change, sign (A) which normally introduces a D.N.
and the D.N. suffix under period glyphs.

On underside	[9.12. 9. 8. 1]	5 *Imix* 4 *Mac*
A1–C1, E1	2. 2. 7. 0	count forward to
F1–E2	[9.14.11.15. 1]	3 *Imix* 14 *Ch'en*

The dates fall respectively in A.D. 680 and A.D. 723. The remaining
glyphs, including several portraits of gods, terminate with a glyph

reading night-shield jaguar, the name glyph of either an individual ruler or, more probably, a dynasty at Yaxchilan (M2) and the so-called emblem glyph of Yaxchilan (N2), perhaps a dynastic title – Lord Owner of (*ah nal*, superfix and suffix, p. 65) the cleft sky. Conceivably the affix at left signifies *halach*, Great Commander, term for Maya rulers.

Some D.N.s are subtractions. The count glyph then exchanges the 'forward' prefix for a second postfix which is, in fact, the D.N. suffix proclaiming reversed order. We think of this as subtraction, but more probably the compound indicates the earlier of linked dates, for at times it follows a date to which an addition is to be made (Fig. 6 *g, h*), but subtraction could also be shown by prefixing an affix resembling a worm or snake to the day from which the count backward was made (Fig. 6 *i*).

In measuring the synodical revolution of Venus the Maya showed their greatest skill. Tables in *Dresden Codex* give multiples of that period averaged to 584 days with amazingly accurate corrections to take care of the overlap of 0·08 days. Five pages follow, each covering calendrical, religious and astrological matters for one of the five days on which the planet's heliacal rising after inferior conjunction 'officially' fell (in fact, it wobbled some three days either side of 583.92 days). Venus was extremely dangerous at those times; certain categories of life were its victims – struck by its light, the Aztec said. In *Dresden Codex* and in books from Central Mexico the Venus gods are painted hurling their spears, that is their death rays (a charming parallel to kids' science fiction). The speared victims – warriors, nobles, crops (represented by the maize god and the earth aspect of Itzam Na) and rainfall (a turtle god, for the turtle symbolized the rains) – are also depicted.

Page 46 of *Dresden Codex* lists stations of the Venus revolution which ended with heliacal rising on a day *Kan*. At the top of the right side of the page the regent of the period is depicted (Pl. 1). The middle picture is of the Venus god regnant on those *Kan* days, a little known deity called God L. He has hurled his spear but still holds his spear-thrower in upraised left hand. The victim, with spear driven into his stomach, is in the bottom picture. He is the earth aspect of Itzam Na, greatest of Maya gods, symbolizing fertility and crops.

The key text of twelve glyph blocks, between top and middle pictures, tells what is in store for mankind. Reading is in pairs top to bottom, first the three pairs on left, 1–6; then those on right, 7–12:

1: *il* affix with hand and lunar action signs. *Il* is the root of a verb to see, with the whole probably meaning something like 'he has been seen.' 2: (in) the east. 3: God L. 4: (is) the great or red Venus. 5: the earth manifestation of Itzam Na. 6: (is) the sacrificial (victim). 7: woe (*numya*) to ?. 8: woe to mankind. 9: the pestilence or punishment of (*u koch*). 10: the abundance of food. 11: woe to the maize god. 12: woe to ?.

Note the bracket, *u*, here used as the possessive whereas previously we saw it employed to form an ordinal (p. 75).

A chant with food offerings to the four great Chacs, the rain gods, crosses the middle of page 30 into the left column of page 31 of *Dresden Codex* (Pl. 5). These gods were at the four sides or angles of the world, each being named for the colour of his world direction. They are associated with days 65 days (note 3 dots [3 × 20] above 5 dots) apart in the sacred almanac of 260 days. As this is a re-entering cycle, the last day recorded, 8 *Chicchan*, is the start of the count: 8 *Chicchan*+65 =8 *Oc*+65 =8 *Men*+65 =8 *Ahau*+65 =8 *Chicchan*. Unusually, there are no pictures. Each compartment (*t'ol*) holds eight glyphs read in pairs top to bottom:

T'ol 1: 1, with *kal*, action, postfix, perhaps *uinan*, set up in order. 2, (in) the east. 3, the red god. 4, an offering of, *holil* (see Fig. 5 *h* for homonym). 5, maize and venison (tamales? or stew?. Note the leg of a deer with cloven hoof). 6, Chac, literally, maker of life. 7, fresh (*bil* suffix) maize. 8, his food or eating (*u hanal*). 8 *Oc* the day.

T'ol 2: 1, set up?. 2, (in) the north. 3, the white god. 4, Chac. 5, turkey. 6, fresh maize. 7, red?. 8, his food. 8 Men the day.

T'ol 3: 1, set up?. 2, (in) the west. 3, the black god. 4, Chac. 5, iguana and maize (dish). 6, fresh maize. 7, black honey?. 8, (his) food. 8 *Ahau* the day.

T'ol 4: 1, set up?. 2, (in) the south. 3, the yellow god. 4, Chac. 5, fish. 6, upon maize. 7, fresh green maize. 8, his food. 8 *Chicchan* the day.

The reading black honey for *T'ol* 3, Glyph 7 is very dubious. It might mean the black sprinklers.

Page 40, middle, of *Dresden Codex* shows *T'ol* 7 to 9 of a long agricultural almanac (Pl. 6). No days are named because the arrangement calls for five day names in each *t'ol*, and there was no room for them. They were calculated from the column of five days at the start of the almanac, the black bars and dots giving the intervals (the red numbers are those of the suppressed day names). The last glyph or glyphs give prognostications for the days in question.

T'ol 7: Picture, a Chac, with axe, his attribute, dives earthward from the sky (a stylized section of the iguana body of Itzam Na, which formed the sky, set with celestial signs – here sky and darkness). The axe is the thunderbolt so launched by the Chacs.

1, in the heart of the heavens (literally, on high). 2, (is) Chac. 3, the maize god. 4, abundance of maize.

T'ol 8: Picture, Kinich Kakmo, Sun Face Fire Macaw, a deity of drought and great heat, strides beneath the sky, a blazing torch, heat and drought symbol, in each hand.

1, His (referable to Glyph 3) fire. 2, there on high. 3, Kinich Kakmo (number 4 here stands for Kinich, the sun god because the sun is god of that number, p. 58). 4 *kintunyaabil*, drought. The elements *kin*, *tun* and *yaab* (*u haab* becomes *yaab*) are present, but the affix *il* is suppressed.

T'ol 9: Picture, a dog with maize plant on head and blazing torch in paw dives from the sky. *Pek*, the general term for dog, also means unfavourable weather, in fact drought. *Pek*, dog, stands for *pek* weather.

1, the sparking torch ?? of. 2, *pek* weather (in) the sky. 3, woe to the (maize) god. 4, woe to the maize seed. Note seed glyph, often combined with earth sign to form the ideogram milpa, corn patch (Fig. 4 *b*, *c*), but here with maize superfix.

Part of an almanac (*Dresden*, p. 16, bottom) shows the moon goddess in her roles of patroness of medicine, diseases and childbirth (Pl. 7). There is a play on words: *koch* means both bear on shoulders and disease or divine punishment – the same thing, for disease was divine punishment. The pictures of birds perched on the goddess's shoulders are a case of rebus illustration. The spiral glyph corresponds to *koch*, perhaps because *koch* signifies bent or twisted in Palencano Chol. The red numbers of the day signs are suppressed.

T'ol 1: Picture, the moon goddess bears on her shoulders (*koch*) the Yucatan screech owl, of very evil disposition. Throughout Middle America owls betoken death. In some parts they are thought to bring all diseases; in others to be the messengers of the death god or to take souls to the place of interment. The Yucatan screech owl, the bird here depicted, is above all of ill omen. Its Maya name is *ah coo akab*, the mad one of the night, but archaeologists refer to it as *Muan* because it represents the month of that name. Here as the *koch*, sent by the moon goddess, it may stand for madness of the patient or evil in general.

1, Glyph of *ah coo akab*; the number 13 refers to the fact that it was perched above the 13 heavens. 2, *u koch ti*, his perched on, but also divine punishment of. 3, *Colel*, Mistress, title of moon goddess. 4, her evil.

T'ol 2: Picture, the moon goddess bears on her shoulders (*koch*) a quetzal.

1, *kuk*, quetzal, but here to be read as its homonym, a metaphor for child or children (*kuk*, sprout, by extension child). 2, *u kaz*, her evil. That is the normal meaning, but in view of Glyph 4 it cannot apply here. Instead, the homonym sexual organs or semen is indicated – the generative powers of. 3, *Colel*, Mistress. 4, very good tidings (*ox*, three, used as a superlative, compare Elizabethan thrice happy, threblefold). The *koch* glyph is omitted presumably because there is no disease or punishment.

T'ol 3: Picture, the moon goddess bears on her shoulders a macaw. *mo*, a term applied to a long series of spasms and seizures.

1, macaw, *mo* seizure. 2, left, the head probably defines the seizure; right, *koch ti*, perched on or disease from. 3, *zac* or *zacal*, white or weave, woman, preferably the latter because the moon goddess was patroness of weaving. 4, *u kaz*, its evil.

Three *t'ol* of another almanac concerned with the moon goddess (*Dresden*, pp. 19–20, bottom; Plate 8) show her with various burdens (*cuch*) on her back, again rebus writing and painting for *cuch* means both back burden and fate. There is a play on sounds, *cuch* with *koch* on the adjacent page.

T'ol 1: Picture, the goddess's back burden is the impersonator of evil (*kaz*).
1, a death and war god, Q (ten, the number corresponding to death, is part of his name) personifies the evil manikin in the picture. 2, the divine burden – fate of (the little *cauac* stands for *ku*, divine). 3, Lady Weaver. 4, affliction of war (wood and stone point affixes are a metaphor for war, p. 49).

T'ol 2: Picture, the moon goddess's *cuch* is the fire symbol, *kak*, here to be read as its homonym *kak*, a term covering various pox diseases.
1, *kak*, here pox diseases. 2, Lady Weaver. 3, divine burden of death?. 4, divine wrath.

T'ol 3: Picture, same *kaz* of *T'ol* 1 is her *cuch*.
1, the death god. 2, the divine burden – fate of. 3, Lady Weaver. 4, much death.

Here the *cuch* is dire in all three *t'ols*.

These exercises in decipherment bring out the overwhelming importance of rebus writing. With a limited number of signs neither alphabetic nor syllabic, such a system was essential for an adequate expression of ideas, and largely monosyllabic Maya was well suited to the method. Context informed the priest what meaning to attach to a given word or verbal root; circumlocution (use of *kuk*, quetzal, for child is a good example) was often necessary.

References

Literature on Maya writing is vast. Below are listed general works and those to which reference is made in the text.

Barthel, T. S. 1955. Maya-Palaeographik: die Hieroglyphe Strafe. *Ethnos*, 20 : 146–51. Stockholm.

Knorozov, Y. V. 1955. *La escritura de los antiguos mayas (ensayo de descifrado) sic*. Institute of Ethnography, Academy of Sciences of U.S.S.R., Moscow.

Landa, D. de. *c*. 1566. *Relación de las cosas de Yucatán*. MS. see Tozzer, A. M.

Maudslay, A. P. 1889–1902. *Archaeology*. Biologia Centrali-americana. 5 vols. London.

—— 1898. A Maya calendar inscription interpreted by Goodman's tables. *Proc. Royal Soc.*, 62 : 67–80. London.

Morley, S. G. 1915. *An introduction to the study of the Maya hieroglyphs*. U.S. Bureau of American Ethnology, Bulletin 57. Washington.

Roys, R. L. 1933. *The Book of Chilam Balam of Chumayel*. Carnegie Institution of Washington Publ. 438. Washington, and (1967) Univ. of Oklahoma Press, Norman.

—— 1965. *Ritual of the Bacabs*. Transl. and ed. Univ. of Oklahoma Press, Norman.

Satterthwaite, L. 1965. Calendrics of the Maya lowlands. *Handbook of Middle American Indians*, 3 : 603–31. Austin.

Swadesh, M. 1961. Interrelaciones de las lenguas mayenses. *Instituto Nacional de Antropología e Historia, Anales*, 13 : 231–67. Mexico.

Thompson, J. E. S. 1950. *Maya hieroglyphic writing: introduction*. Carnegie Institution of Washington Publ. 589 and (1960) Univ. of Oklahoma Press, Norman.

—— 1962. *A catalog of Maya hieroglyphs*. Univ. of Oklahoma Press, Norman.

—— 1972 *A commentary on the Dresden codex, a Maya hieroglyphic book*. American Philosophical Society, Philadelphia.

Tozzer, A. M. 1941. *Landa's relación de las cosas de Yucatán. A translation edited with notes*. Peabody Museum, Harvard Univ., Papers 18. Cambridge, Mass.

Whorf, B. L. 1933. The phonetic value of certain characters in Maya writing. Peabody Museum, Harvard University, Papers, 13 : 2. Cambridge, Mass.

Zimmermann, G. 1956. *Die Hieroglyphen der Maya-Handschriften*. Univ. of Hamburg Abhandlungen aus dem Gebiet der Auslandskunde 62 – Reihe B. Hamburg.

Index

Numbers in parentheses are those assigned to hieroglyphs in J. E. S. Thompson, *A catalog of Maya hieroglyphs*. University of Oklahoma Press. Norman, 1962.

Calendar
Almanac, 260-day, 21, 23, 25, 27, 49, 61–63, 76–80
Computations, 70–72
Correlation with Christian, 23–24
Day signs (additional to fig. 7), *Ahau* (533), 73, 78, frontispiece; *Chicchan* (726), 78; *Ik* (503), 53; *Imix* (501), 52, 69, 75; *Ix* (524), 22, 59; *Lamat* (510a), 75; *Manik* (671), 63; *Men* (613), 78; *Muluc* (513), 56, 59; *Oc* (567), 78
Distance numbers, 74–76; suffix, (126), 75
Initial Series, 24, 70–74
Journey of time, 55
Lunar count, 70–74
Month signs (additional to fig. 8), *Ch'en,* (95.60:528), 66, frontispiece; *Kankin* (559), 74; *Mac* (74:625), 51; *Muan* (748), 74; *Uo* (95:552), 74; *Yax* (16:528), 74; *Yaxkin* (16:544.116), 35, 74; *Zac* (58.528), 71; *Zip* (109:552), 72–73
Starting point, 24, 70

Hieroglyphs, General Considerations
Affixes, 9, 28–30, 66–67
Alphabet, 31–32
Arrangement, textual, 27
Attributive, 51, 57
Books, 24–25, 30
Catalogues 35
Clauses 67, 72
Compound, 28, 35
Computerized, 34
Cursive, 30
Decipherment, 25, 31–35, 49, 51
Determinatives, 49, 57–58
Development, 20–24
Emblem, 65, 76
Expansion, 66
Fluidity, 28
Full figure, 59, frontispiece

Homonyms, 47–50, 54, 59, 66, 67, 71–72, 78–80
Ideograms, 51–53, 64
Infixes, 66, 71
Limitations, 60, 68, 80
Main signs, 9, 28–29, 67
Metaphorgrams, 49, 53, 55–56, 71, 80
Non-Maya, 20, 22, 28
Number of, 9
Numbers, 59, 70–76, 80
Origins, 20–24
Pars pro toto, 59
Phonetic, 32–34. *See also* Homonyms
Portrait, 9, 29, 58–59, 61–63, 72–74
Punning, 50, 60–61, 80
Reading order, 27–28
Rebus writing, *see* Homonyms
Ruler's, 76
Rules of composition, 35–67
Speech, correspondence to, 22, 35, 48, 50–51, 55, 63
Suppression of elements, 64–66, 74, 78
Syllabic, 33
Symbolic, 61, 78
Synonyms, 51
T'ol defined, 27

Hieroglyphs, Individual
Ah, masculine, (168) 64; with *nal,* lord, owner, 65, 76
Al (23), 30, 35, 60, 67, 71–72
Axe, *baat* (190), 63, 73, 78
Backward (126 and 206), 59, 76
Bak, meat, terror (558), 49
Baktun, 400-*tun* period (528.528:60), 70–73
Balche, mead, forest denizen (283), 58
Bat (756), 51, 55–56, 65, 66
Bil, vegetal growth, participial suffix (130), 29, 53, 54, 60–61, 65, 78
Black, *ek* (95), 29, 66, 78
Ca, comb element (25), 61, 64, 71
Caan, sky (561), 35, 56, 60, 73
Cab, earth, honey (526:251), 51, 56, 58, 73
Cacao, chocolate (25:25.130), 61
Cauac, storm, god, divine (528), 35, 48, 57, 64, 66, 71, 73
Chac, red, great (109), 57, 73, 77 ,78
Chac, rain god (668.103), 78

Coc, turtle shell, misery (626), 51
Comb, *see Ca*
Conch shell (210), 57
Cord (116), 64, 66, 71
Cotton, hank of (145), 57
Cuch, back burden, destiny, seat of office
   (601), 49, 55, 57, 60, 80
Deer hoof, *mai* (294), 59–60
Dog, *see Pek*
Dz'a, give (667), 54
East (534:544.116), 77
Feminine prefix, *x* (1026), 35
Fish, *cai* (203), 64, 70; prefix (204), 64
Foot (301), 32
Forward (679), 59, 75
Frog or toad (741), 63, 73
Frog or toad, upturned (740), 72
Haab, year (528:116), 29, 64, 75, 78
Halach, he who commands (Affixes
   36–40?), 76
Hanal, eat (1038b), 52–53, 78
Hand, 53, 63, 73
Hatzcab, dawn (561:544:526), 56, 59
Heart, *see Pucsikal*
Hel, change (573), 75
Hidz', expiration (12), 64
Hol, offering, head, end (585a), 77
Iguana, (799), 78
Il, relationship, see (24), 29, 30, 35, 60,
   77, 78
Jade, water (513), 56, 59, 75
Jaguar paw, war, *chacmol* (234), 60
Jaguar skin, night sky, rulership (609),
   55, 65, 71, frontispiece
Kak, fire, pox, ebony (563), 48–50, 80
Kal, twenty, action (181), 54–55, 64, 77
Kan, maize (506), 52, 60–61, 78
Kan, yellow (281), 78
Katun, 20-*tun* period (28:548), 70–75
Kaz, evil, halfway (648), 50, 79, 80
Kin, sun, day, festival (544.116), 29, 35,
   56, 57, 64, 65, 70–75, 78
Kintun, excessive sun (544.548), 66
Kintunyaabil, drought (544:528.548:24),
   29, 47, 78
Koch, disease, bear on shoulders (19), 60,
   77, 79–80
Ku, god, divine (528), 35, 48, 57, 80

Kuk, quetzal offspring (604.604), 79
Mac, turtle carapace (626), 51
Macaw seizure, *mo* (744), 79
Maize, *see Kan;* affix 85, 79
Malevolent, *lob* (267), 66
Mankind, *uinicil* (521:103), 77
Mat (614), 49, 57
Men, craftsman (612 and 613), 57
Milpa, corn field (526:251.663:23), 51
Moon (683), 55, 63–64, 72
Muan bird (748), 79
North (23.1037), 78
Numya, woe (172), 77–79
Pack, merchants (680), 57, 72
Pek, dog, bad weather (559.568), 33, 78
Puczikal, heart, sacrifice (567), 47, 51, 52.
   66, 77
Red, *see Chac*
Sacrifice, *see Puczikal*
Seating (644), 66
Seed (663), 51, 79
Shield (624), 55
South (134.74:17.134), 78
Stone point (112), 49, 80. *See also Tun*
Tab, cord (60), 67
Tan, toward, time (74), 29
Tanlah, serve (74:669), 54, 60
Te or *che,* wood etc. (87), 48–49, 57, 71
Ti or *ta,* at, in, from, excrement (59),
   66–67, 75
Tun, year, stone, excessive (548), 24, 29,
   35, 60, 70–74, 78
Turkey (839), 78
Turtle carapace (626), 51, 76
Tzil, revered (103), 53
U, of, his (1), 30, 60, 75, 77–80
Uinal, 20-day month (521), 63, 70–75
Very good tidings (111.567:130), 79
Vulture (747), 66–67
Water, *see Jade*
West (219:544.116), 78
Woe, *see Numya*
Xoc, shark, count (738), 59, 75
Yax, green, new, strong (16 and 17), 29,
   30, 35, 48, 59, 60, 62
Yol, heart of, offering (96), 58, 78
Zac, white, fear, weave (58), 50, 71
Zaca, maize drink (58.33:506), 52

Names and Associations of Deities

Bacabs, 30, 51, 57, 62
Bolonyocte, 48
Chacs, 53, 62, 77–78
Chicchans, 62
Death, 58, 62, 73, 74
Earth, 53, 58, 62
Itzam Na, 53, 62, 72, 76–78
Ix Chebel Yax, 57
Jaguar, 58, 62

Kinich Kakmo, 78
Maize, 58, 62, 76
Merchant, 48, 57, 72
Moon, 58, 62, 73, 79–80, frontispiece
Nine lords of nights, 67, 70, 74, frontispiece
Sacrifice, 62
Sun, 58, 62, 65, 71, 73, 74, 78
Venus, 62, 71, 76–77
War, 80